MW01713850

# 60'6"

## Balls, Strikes, and Baseball Mortality

Drew,

Best of luck on your career! Enjoy the story!

Mik[illegible]

*For my parents*

# 60'6"

## Balls, Strikes, and Baseball Mortality

a novel

Mike Arsenault

GSPH

GSPH

GENERAL STORE PUBLISHING HOUSE
499 O'Brien Road, Box 415
Renfrew, Ontario, Canada K7V 4A6
Telephone 1.613.432.7697 or 1.800.465.6072
www.gsph.com

ISBN 978-1-926962-40-5



Cover art, design, formatting: Magdalene Carson
Printed by Custom Printers of Renfrew Ltd., Renfrew, Ontario
Printed and bound in Canada



Library and Archives Canada Cataloguing in Publication
Arsenault, Mike, 1985-
60'6" : balls, strikes, and baseball mortality / Mike Arsenault.
ISBN 978-1-926962-40-5
I. Title. II. Title: Sixty feet six inches.
PS8601.R7325S59 2011 C813'.6 C2011-907122-3

DISCLAIMER

*60"6': Balls, Strikes, and Baseball Mortality* is a work of fiction. Names, characters, places, and incidents are products of the author's imagination, or have been used fictitiously.
Any resemblance to actual events, locales, or persons, living or dead, is entirely coincidental.

## Acknowledgements

There is a litany of people I want to thank who have supported and helped me through each evolution of this manuscript over the past few years. I'll do this in reverse chronological order, beginning with my book's publication (a very cool phrase to see typed out) and then heading back to my own start in the game of baseball.

Thanks to my publisher, Tim Gordon, my editor, Jane Karchmar, and the rest of the staff at General Store Publishing House for making this dream a reality and navigating me through the many twists and turns (and edits) of publishing a novel.

I would not have found GSPH as a publishing option were it not for the guidance of Morris Dalla Costa and Chip Martin.

Mark Zwolinski and William Humber gave invaluable feedback on early versions of my manuscript and wrote very positive critiques for my query letter. Allan Grozelle offered a multitude of free printing services that was much needed and appreciated. My sister, Malory, provided me with a number of helpful edits and suggestions.

Kate Banks and all of my close friends and family deserve special mention.

This book wouldn't be possible without my parents, Gord and Susan. I want to thank my dad for convincing me that I had the talent to write a book in the first place. It was his idea to write baseball fiction. I want to thank my mom for always being there for me and backing my desire to pursue a career off the beaten path from a typical nine-to-five job.

Last, I want to thank all of my past teammates and coaches who have inspired the concoction of stories and characters that created *60"6': Balls, Strikes, and Baseball Mortality*, from my humble beginnings in the Oshawa Minor Baseball Association, to my post-secondary career at Queen's University and Durham College, my summer seasons in the Ontario Senior Baseball Association and the Greater Toronto Baseball League, and finally to the London Majors of the Intercounty Baseball League.

# July 2008

## Dunedin, Florida

The dream was always the same.

Every April, like clockwork, it grabbed hold of his subconscious and dominated his nights until the summer sun was forced from the sky and replaced by crisp autumn winds.

April to September. Baseball season. Every year since 1997. The year he turned thirteen. The year he became a pitcher.

For Gord Mattis, the dream was both a blessing and a curse. A curse because it scared him. It kept him awake at night, his breath short, his heart palpitating like a jackhammer, and his body slick with cold sweat. A blessing because without it, he felt lost. Like a man without a purpose. He thought the dream defined who he was.

The dream was always the same.

> *Gord opens his eyes and finds himself on the loneliest hill in the world. Ten inches of dirt and clay. The pitcher's mound. Fifty thousand pairs of eyes bear down on him, like they're trying to peer into his soul.*
>
> *He grabs the resin bag and feels the fine powder cling to his sweat-soaked hands and forearms. He tosses it once in the air and flings it to the back of the mound. He slowly rubs the white pearl in both hands, tracing the stitching and cowhide leather with his fingertips.*
>
> *Taking a hip-width stance on the rubber, Gord squares his shoulders and wipes his left spike across an imaginary undulation in the dirt in front of him. He focuses his gaze on the hitter, sixty feet six inches away.*
>
> *Both the hitter and the crowd are faceless. It's just Gord and the mitt—a tempestuous relationship that, when working, can be a form of artistic perfection.*

*He steps back with his right foot to start his balanced, mechanically efficient delivery that's been honed through thousands of repetitions and hundreds of hours of practice.*

*But something's wrong.*

*The motion is anything but smooth. His joints flail wildly, like they're attached to a puppeteer's strings. Gord tries to regain control of his limbs, but his body ignores his brain. He has lost complete control. A sick feeling develops in the pit of his stomach. The wretched taste of bile burns his esophagus.*

*The wild gyrations continue as Gord's left arm comes forward at an obscene angle and attempts to release the ball toward the mitt. The result is a cross between a shot put and a five-year-old flinging a mosquito off her shoulder.*

*The ball lands fifteen feet in front of the plate and rolls toward the batter, who stops it with his left foot. Boos and catcalls rain down from every corner of the stadium. Gord gets the ball back and, with great trepidation, tries another pitch. This time the delivery is even more awkward. The ball loops over the batter's head and strikes the base of the backstop, fifty feet from home plate.*

*Again and again, Gord's pitches fly all over the park—some falling short, some going too long, others thrown halfway up the baselines. None come close to the strike zone.*

*He's powerless to stop it. The crowd's taunts become more derisive and vitriolic. The boos thunder down onto the field and rattle his eardrums.*

*The walks and runs pile up like stacks of cordwood. Gord looks in desperation to the bullpen, longing for relief and an end to the nightmare, but no one is there. He is completely and utterly alone . . .*

Gord Mattis jolted awake. Disoriented, he was unsure of where he was. The motel room sheets clung to his body like paper towel on a wet counter. A cool sea breeze drifted in through the oceanfront window, tickling his nostrils and slowing his frantic breathing.

The soothing sounds of waves breaking against the beach jogged Gord's memory and brought him back to the present. He peered through the darkness and recognized the decrepit seediness of his double room at the Motel 6 in Dunedin.

A glance at the alarm clock revealed the time: 2:30 a.m.

Gord noticed that his roommate's bed was empty. The sheets and comforter were packed with a military-like precision, typical of a motel housecleaning service. *Danny must still be out trolling for ass.*

He shuffled into the bathroom and flipped on the light. He shut his eyes tight, waiting for his sight to acclimate to the brightness. The glare off the blinding white tile in the tiny, mildew-stained bathroom shook the remaining fog from his mind.

He gazed at himself in the mirror. Brown, shaggy hair and four days' worth of stubble stared back at him. At six feet two inches and 215 pounds, Gord possessed a strong, muscular physique that was the envy of the rest of the pitching staff on the Lakeland Wildcats of the Class A Central Florida League.

Unfortunately, the so-called "Steroid Era" had unfairly painted all clean ballplayers with the same brush as the drug cheats who had cheapened the integrity of America's pastime. Doubts were cast and eyebrows rose anytime a player, especially a pitcher, showed up at spring training with a body typically seen gracing the cover of *Men's Health*.

Whispers of performance-enhancing drug use dogged many players. For many fans and media members, it was now "guilty until proven innocent." The proliferation of sports blogs and the lack of accountability on the Internet made the outlandish claims and wild accusations of PED use all the more prevalent.

But Gord Mattis never used steroids, unlike so many of his fellow athletes. His musculature was the result of hours spent in the weight room and not as a trustee of modern chemistry.

Gord shut off the bathroom light. He made slow, methodical circles with his left arm, hoping to loosen his joints and release the shoulder stiffness that had built up throughout the night. The cracking in his shoulder and the barking in his elbow were vestigial duress from his pitching appearance the night before. It was nothing new;

just typical wear and tear on a limb not meant to throw objects overhand at high velocity.

Crawling back into bed, Gord heard two voices outside the room.

"What, what house—room, heh heh, are you in?" An obviously drunk woman.

"1–0 . . . 3. No, no 3 . . . 0–1," was a man's slurred reply.

Gord smiled, recognizing his roommate's voice. *Sounds like Danny was successful.*

This was something Gord had to put up with on a fairly regular basis. Danny Johnson, his roommate, was an eighteen-year-old fireballer from Oklahoma City. He was the Detroit organization's newest bonus baby. Blessed with a ninety-seven mile an hour fastball, Johnson was snapped up sixth overall in the June draft and signed for a cool $7 million. A month earlier, Danny pitched in his last high school game. Now he was in Single A ball, fucking his way up and down the Gulf Coast.

Gord, at twenty-four, was the oldest member of the Lakeland Wildcats and in his second year with the club. Not blessed with overwhelming stuff, he depended on location, command, and deception to succeed on the hill.

The rest of the Wildcats' roster was comprised primarily of high round draft picks not yet able to drink legally in the continental United States. Being the senior member of any minor league team was never a good thing. Gord might as well have worn a scarlet letter on his chest. Twenty-four-year-old Single A lefties were not highly regarded on any organization's depth chart.

Tom Conrad, Lakeland's manager, had roomed them together thinking that Gord would be a maturing presence to the callow flamethrower. Unfortunately, possessing maturity in a professional baseball clubhouse is akin to being the best-smelling turd in a shit pile. It was a sliding scale.

Danny and his new friend stumbled loudly through the door and entered the motel room.

"Make yourssssssellllfffff comfur—comfurble, Lauren."

"Lauren? My name's Lindsay."

"Oh, yeah." He whispered an aside to himself, "Like it matters."

Lindsay, oblivious or unwilling to recognize Danny's callous comment, noticed Gord, with his back to the pair, lying on the bed farthest from the door.

"You didn't tell me you had a roommate! I'm not sleeping with you with someone else in the room."

"No, he's cool. A real deep sleeper. Watch this: Hey, Gord! You awake? Gord?"

This dialogue was a regular occurrence. A few times a week, Danny returned to their room with his newest conquest. Upon seeing Gord in the next bed, said conquest would express concerns that the night would devolve into some type of sexual handicap match. Gord, whether he was awake or not, stayed silent to assuage her fears.

Gord, ever the devoted wingman, ignored Danny's provocations. He quickly fell into a light sleep, and the couple romped around the open bed in a drunken stupor.

Ninety minutes later, Gord's sleep was disrupted once again. Not from the dream, the sea breeze, or the waves, but from two strange sounds.

Squeak.

Thwap.

Squeak.

Thwap.

Squeak.

Thwap.

Squeak.

Thwap.

Squeak.

Thwap.

The two bizarre sounds, building in crescendo, alternated back and forth like volleys in a tennis match until Gord, forced by curiosity, rolled over to take a look.

It would have been smarter to remain curious. Gord saw a stark naked Danny perched above an equally naked Lindsay like a peregrine falcon trying to feed its young from an elevated position. Danny's blindingly pale, white ass drilled away at the poor girl like an offshore rig trying to strike oil.

Besides the obvious, the oddest thing about the scene was how quiet Lindsay was. Danny was panting like a steam engine, and she was as quiet as a mouse. Gord furrowed his brow and smirked quizzically. *Danny Boy may be able to throw a baseball through a brick wall, but it sounds like he could use a little more lead in his pencil.*

Gord quietly slipped out of bed and took a comforter and pillow out to the balcony. He paused at the sliding glass door as the warm sea air fluttered the heavy polyester drapes. He heard a soft moan from underneath the Oklahoma Oil Rig. He nodded approvingly. *Good, she's alive. We don't have to add necrophilia to Danny's ever-increasing list of off-field exploits.*

He settled into the cheap plastic chair and slid the glass door shut. Attempting to position himself as comfortably as possible, he smiled inwardly. *Oh, the glamorous life of a minor league ballplayer.*

The next morning, Gord squinted through the first slivers of the Florida sun peeking over the horizon. He ran barefoot along the surf near the motel as the fledgling sunlight warmed the cool perspiration blanketing his forehead and chest. The wet, goopy sand squished beneath his feet and kicked up behind him like a dirt bike tearing around a mud track.

Every hundred yards, Gord abruptly dropped to the sand and knocked out a set of twenty push-ups. The pulsating rhythms of the classic rock exploding out of his iPod kept his intensity high and forced him to finish the workout.

The daily run and push-up routine was just one of many mechanisms Gord used to stay in peak physical condition. His rigorous training routines coupled strength work with metabolic conditioning and were used to squeeze every last mile per hour out of his left arm, which topped out at eighty-seven on a good day.

He climbed the concrete steps of the motel, shaded a putrid pastel pink, and made his way back to the room. Not surprised to see that Lindsay was nowhere to be found, he set down a tray of coffees, which he had picked up from the lobby, on the dresser next to the cheap television.

"Hey, Sunshine, wake up. Where'd your little friend go?"

A grunt sounded from under the sheet.

"From the brief look I got of her, you may want to pick up a gallon of cranberry juice on our way out."

"Fuck off."

"I'm just saying, if it burns when you pee, you might want to rethink your current recruitment strategy."

Danny ignored the jab. "What time is it?"

"Just after eight. We have to be at the community centre at nine."

Manager Tom Conrad was a reformed alcoholic who gave himself to the Lord after his first marriage disintegrated in 1995. Now Born Again and a devout Baptist, Conrad had only two goals in his life: to commit himself to the betterment of the world and to win ball games. At 23–35, the Lakeland Wildcats fell well short of the latter, so Conrad made it his personal mission to ensure his team would achieve the former.

Every off-day, while other Central Florida League teams were sleeping away their hangovers till the early afternoon, Conrad would have the Wildcats up early volunteering at soup kitchens, helping inner city youth, teaching primary school kids how to read—which proved to be problematic for some of Lakeland's more intellectually challenged players—and other like endeavours.

That morning, the team was scheduled to appear at Highbury Park from nine to twelve helping young baseball players master the fine arts of the game. Attendance, as always, was mandatory. Even a bonus baby like Danny Johnson was forced to attend these excursions. Conrad said they "built character" and would be good for the players' "spiritual selves." Danny usually just tried to keep quiet and not vomit all over himself.

After a quick shower to wash off the dried sand clinging to his body, Gord emerged from the bathroom to find Danny, flirting with coherence, sitting on the edge of his bed trying to steady his hands long enough to take a sip of bitter motel coffee.

"So are you going to see . . . uh . . . what was her name again?"

"Linda." Danny shook his head. "Naw, man. Fuck and chuck. She was terrible. I think she might have been a virgin."

"Yeah, I'm sure she has always longed to have her first time be in a Motel 6 with a drunken jackass like you."

"Whatever, man. I gave her an option. Mouth or vagina. She chose B."

A bewildered smile crossed Gord's face. "You are all class, my friend."

The sprawling complex at Highbury Park would have made Ray Kinsella rethink his declaration that an Iowa cornfield was baseball heaven. Five fully equipped diamonds shone like emeralds against the bright Florida sun. The diamonds encircled a synthetic turf field house outfitted with ten batting cages throwing various speeds. The park was meticulously maintained by the city of Dunedin and was a tremendous source of pride for the county.

Two hundred members of the Dunedin Minor Baseball Association were warming up in organized chaos on the field house turf when the Lakeland team bus arrived.

"All right, gentlemen," began Tom Conrad. "There are two hundred kids out there depending on us. They've been looking forward to this day for weeks, so don't let them down. Smile, listen to what they have to say, and help out with not only baseball skills, but life skills."

Nearly inaudible groans reverberated throughout the chartered bus. The team had heard this same speech, in one variation or another, numerous times throughout the year. Unfortunately, the frequency of said speech was inversely proportional to the team's success on the field. With wins few and far between, Conrad appeared to have added life coach and motivational speaker to his on-field duties.

The ten members of the Lakeland pitching staff were sent to one of the adjoining diamonds. There, they saw a group of fifty pitchers between the ages of eight and thirteen, throwing under the watchful gazes of a handful of DMBA coaches.

Each Wildcat was in charge of a group of five kids. The biggest problem that young pitchers faced was the ability to replicate sound mechanics on every pitch. With that in mind, Gord spent the majority of his time with the group dissecting their deliveries in minute detail. He wanted to enforce the importance of developing a consistent landing point with the plant foot and a consistent release point with the throwing arm. Gord knew that mastering those aspects of the delivery was the key to throwing strikes and was the hallmark of a true pitcher.

Unfortunately, mechanical drills were not the tweens' idea of fun, so Gord had to buffer the lesson with games and constant breaks. During one such break, he observed the interactions between his group. The five kids, all twelve years old, were from different teams in the DMBA. There was one right-hander in the group who seemed like somewhat of an outcast. The kid's name was Matthew.

Of average height and about twenty pounds overweight, Matthew was by far the worst pitcher in the group. He had a weak arm and significant trouble with Gord's delivery drills. The other four kids picked up on this incompetence and teased Matthew mercilessly. Their ridicule was just another example of the survival of the fittest mentality in the fierce jungle known as male adolescence.

Something about the situation struck a chord with Gord. Watching the other kids ostracize Matthew solely for being athletically challenged starkly reminded Gord of his own minor baseball experiences. Suddenly he found himself drifting back to the summer of his fourteenth year, a period of time in which Gord's dream of becoming a professional baseball player was not only an immense long shot, but downright laughable.

# May 1998

## Ann Arbor, Michigan
## Concord Field

"BALL FOUR!" the umpire bellowed and pointed a crooked finger to first base. The batter flung his bat toward the visiting team's dugout and jogged down to first, loading the bases.

On the mound, Gord Mattis, three weeks removed from his fourteenth birthday, shook his head in exasperation. Squinting in his oversized, Harry Potter-like glasses, Gord surveyed the situation around him.

Top of the third. Five runs in already, by way of five hits and six walks. Gord had officially lost control of this Washtenaw Amateur Baseball Association league game. The catcher whipped the ball back to Gord as if to say, "Throw a goddamn strike for a change!" It exploded into his mitt, creating a mushroom cloud of dust.

*What a dickhead*, Gord thought. Jason Hamilton, the team's star catcher, coupled tremendous defensive ability with raw hitting power to be the unquestioned top player in the entire WABA under-fifteen league. Unfortunately, Hamilton knew it. He was an egotistical, cocky prick, who felt it was beneath him to catch Gord, the team's worst pitcher by a wide margin.

Hamilton also assumed that it was his duty to remind Gord of this fact on a regular basis. The teasing extended beyond the baseball field to encompass Gord's immense unpopularity among the opposite sex. Oddly enough, fourteen-year-old girls weren't attracted to the thick glasses and short, doughy physique that he possessed.

Time was called as the team manager, Dave Kinsey, slowly trudged to the mound with his hands stuffed in his back pockets. Gord turned to look at his defence as his coach crossed the foul line.

Shortstop Chris Bocking and second baseman Darren Finn were huddled behind second base gesticulating to each other and talking intently. Although Gord couldn't hear what they were saying, their body language and close friendship with Jason Hamilton transmitted the message loud and clear. They were unhappy playing behind Gord, as his starts usually involved a ton of pitches, lots of walks, and a glacial pace of play.

"How's it feel, Gordie?" Kinsey said through gritted teeth.

"I feel fine. I just don't have it today."

"We really need you to throw some strikes, here."

*No shit*, Gord thought. All coaches were the same. They rarely had any good advice to divulge during a mound visit. Their entire occupation was asking pitchers how they felt and imploring them to throw strikes.

*You mean you want me to throw strikes?* Gord wanted to say. *I never thought of that. What a novel idea. What the fuck do you think I've been trying to do?*

Instead, Gord offered a meek reply. "Yes, sir."

"What do *you* think, Jay?"

Jason Hamilton looked Gord up and down with a dismissive sneer. "He's done. Nothing's working."

Kinsey considered his catcher's recommendation. Losing the confidence of your catcher usually sounded the death knell for that outing, and today was no different.

"You know what? I want to stop the bleeding. That's it for today."

Kinsey tapped his right arm, signalling a reliever in from the bullpen. Without a word, Gord placed the ball in his coach's hand and made the seemingly endless, lonely walk to the first base dugout. The parents watching the game engaged in a polite smattering of applause as he vacated the mound, but there was an air of "Thank God *that's* over" in their gesture.

Gord flopped down at the end of the bench and tried to let the sun's harsh rays wash away the memories of what just took place on the field. Some of his teammates walked over and offered half-hearted platitudes like, "Nice job," "Good try," and "Get them next time."

As Gord's replacement threw the last of his warm-up pitches, the team's first base coach sidled beside him and sat down. The coach, Michael Mattis, also doubled as Gord's father.

"You're not throwing enough between outings. I've been telling you that we need to throw long toss and have bullpen sessions at least twice a week. When are you going to start listening to me?"

Gord glared at his father but remained silent.

"We can't keep running you out there like this. This has got to be getting embarrassing for you."

What Michael really meant was embarrassing for *him*. Truthfully, the only reason Gord was even on the under-fifteen WABA travel team was because of his father's close friendship with Dave Kinsey. They had known each other for over twenty years, working for the city of Ann Arbor.

Michael had agreed to be the first base coach because it's an unwritten rule in organized baseball that you are guaranteed a spot on the team if your dad is a coach, no matter how bad at the sport you may be.

And Gord was bad—although a harsher adjective may have done his ineptitude justice. Professional scouts loved to use the word "tools" to describe the physical capabilities of prospective players. A "five-tool" player was a prospect with transcendent talent. Mickey Mantle was a five-tool player, as was Willie Mays. Alex Rodriguez was a contemporary example.

The five tools were the ability to run, hit, hit with power, field, and throw. Of the five, Gord possessed exactly zero. His toolbox was empty.

It was sad, because Gord was absolutely in love with the game of baseball. He ate, slept, and breathed the game. He pored over the newspaper box scores every morning during the season. He voraciously read any book that dealt with the game, and had his eyes and ears glued to any television or radio broadcast. One time, Gord and Michael, not wanting to choose between two games with major post-season implications, watched one game on TV and listened to the other on the radio.

Gord was a true baseball fan, yet, cruelly, possessed sub-marginal skills. As a seven-year-old learning the game, he was actually the top player on his house league team—thanks to having had the finer points of the game drilled into his head by his father from the time he could walk.

And, at that age, anyone who knew the basic rules of the game was the de facto best player. Most kids were more interested in picking blades of grass and drawing in the infield dirt than learning the art of the force out. As these kids were weeded out of organized baseball, Gord slowly tumbled down the talent depth chart as real baseball players flooded into the Ann Arbor minor baseball system.

Furthermore, Gord, as a southpaw, was severely limited in the positions he could play on the field. Coaches initially stuck him in the outfield, as balls rarely left the infield airborne during players' formative years. Once the hairy hands of puberty took hold and balls began tracing high, arcing parabolas in the sky, Gord's inability to track a fly ball led to his banishment to the easiest position on the diamond: first base.

Traditionally, first base was reserved for players with prodigious power and batting averages significantly north of the Mendoza Line—so named for the light-hitting Mario Mendoza, a shortstop who played in the mid-1970s with the Pittsburgh Pirates and whose batting average rarely cracked the .200 plateau. When Gord turned thirteen, and it was evident that a power stroke was not going to reveal itself, his tenuous grip on a WABA travel team roster spot hung by a thread.

Ironically, the saving grace for Gord's "career" was because he was left-handed. The year before, Dave Kinsey, needing a left-handed arm on his staff, put Gord on the hill as a last resort. Surprisingly, he was marginally better as a pitcher than as a position player. It was basically a stay of execution, due to another unwritten rule in minor baseball that a coach will have a left-handed pitcher on the roster no matter how ineffective he may be.

Gord was reminded of this ineffectiveness by the suffocating silence that enveloped the ride home after his disastrous outing.

The silence exacerbated the widening gulf in Michael and Gord's relationship. Michael's disappointment was palpable as it hung in the air with every word that wasn't spoken. Gord looked at his father, waiting to hear at least a modicum of encouragement, but he knew that wait would prove fruitless.

Michael, a former high school star shortstop growing up in Kalamazoo, found it difficult to relate to his son's on-field troubles. Known for his intense competitiveness, Michael shortsightedly tried to light a fire under his son by using the silent treatment and heavily critical, verbal jabs. He hoped it would lead to an improvement in Gord's athletic performance.

But the tactics rarely worked. Although Gord became angry at his father, enhanced skill was not the result. Their mutual love of the game bonded them and threatened to tear them apart. Every spring and summer, they spent dozens of hours on the ball field working on Gord's skill development. Michael would throw hundreds of batting practice pitches and hit even more ground balls. Baseball was their father-and-son bonding time.

Unfortunately, their bonding never mimicked the tear-jerking scene at the end of *Field of Dreams*. Usually, Michael, fed up with the lack of progress, and Gord, sick of Michael's criticize-first teaching approach, would infuriate one another to the point that the practice session dissolved into one of their legendary shouting matches.

Of course, since they were both males, Michael and Gord had lightning-fast rebound rates and they'd be back on the field the next day, and the cycle would repeat itself.

Gord was filled with dread as he pictured the inevitable workout that was sure to follow such a desultory performance. Michael parked the minivan in the family's driveway and erased the cone of silence surrounding the vehicle.

"Don't forget your gear." He took off up the driveway and into the Mattis's modest two-bedroom bungalow. Gord was left to reflect on yet another failed outing in the sport he loved.

# July 2008

## Lakeland, Florida
## Mercantile Stadium

"Gord."

"GORDOOO!"

Slumped against the side of his locker, Gord was jarred from his daydream by the shrill, high-pitched voice of Lakeland's third baseman, Tyson Dante. At five feet six and 145 pounds, Dante resembled a jockey in the Kentucky Derby rather than a major leaguer prospect, but the kid could flat-out hit. His average had never dipped below .350 at any point in his life. Currently, in his first year of A ball, he was humming along at a .358 clip. Growing up in the baseball mecca of Southern California, the worst average of Dante's high school career was .520.

Initially dismissed because of his diminutive stature, Dante had something of a Napoleon complex. A short fuse, coupled with an abrasive personality, made him a polarizing figure in the Wildcats' clubhouse. When Dante was hitting well, he was a great guy. But, if he was struggling or, God forbid, went hitless in a game, then it was best to keep your distance. The shards of smashed bats that littered Lakeland's clubhouse floor and the dents in the walls could attest to that.

"What do you want, Lilliputian?"

"Where did you—what do you keep calling me 'Lilliputian' for? What does that mean?"

Baseball players were considered to be some of the dumbest athletes on the planet. A lot of them went straight to the minor leagues from high school, bypassing a college education completely. And Dante was basically an idiot savant. He was a genius when it came to the art of hitting. He could spend hours talking your ear off about his craft, but he was completely useless in social situations or intelligent discourse. For Gord, it was like having his very own *Rain Man*.

Baseball wasn't exactly rocket science. Hockey and basketball at least required technical proficiency and the memorization of set plays and schemes. At its root, baseball was essentially a Cro-Magnon exploit: See ball. Hit ball. Catch ball.

"It's from a show on MTV." Gord decided it was best not to confuse his bewildered teammate. "I think I saw it on *Cribs*."

"Oh. Okay. Cool. That's a sweet show."

"What did you want, Ty?"

"Did you move my spikes?"

Gord glanced at Dante's locker and noticed his teammate's spikes lying slightly askew in front of his pock-marked wooden stool.

"Your spikes are right there," Gord said, pointing to Dante's worn, dark blue Mizunos.

The cleats had seen better days and they smelled like an open carton of milk curdling on a windowsill in late August. Dante thought the spikes brought him luck, hence his reticence to get a new pair. The rest of the team pretended the rank odour didn't exist, so long as Dante kept ripping the cover off the ball.

"Yeah, I know, but they're in the wrong spot."

Gord was exasperated. "What the fuck are you talking about?"

"Each shoe has to be pointed toward the centre of the clubhouse, exactly a batting glove width apart. The laces have to be tucked into each shoe with the top eyelet empty. Look at them. They're all over the place!"

Each spike was pointed toward the other at a forty-five-degree angle. A wisp of the left spike lace flopped haphazardly on the cement clubhouse floor. Gord, a wry smile playing across his face, looked back at Dante.

"I guess I nudged them when I was looking for my iPod. Please accept my sincerest apologies."

Dante was undeterred. "That's not good enough, Gord. If my spikes aren't in the right place when I come in, I can't hit that game." A light bulb flashed on in Tyson's head. "THAT'S why I went 1 for 4 last night!"

Gord stood up to leave, lest he be forced to listen to an in-depth, pitch-by-pitch analysis of Dante's previous night's at-bats. Once Tyson got going, he was impossible to stop. After fifteen minutes of such mind-numbing minutiae, the poor soul stuck in the conversation would be searching for an ice pick to jab into his brainstem.

"Where are you going?" Dante asked.

Gord turned and flashed a shit-eating grin. "To shag flies. Someone has to catch those droopy Texas leaguers you float into the outfield every batting practice."

Dante bent down to reconfigure his spikes. "Fuck you."

It was days like this that reaffirmed Gord's love for the game of baseball. The cloudless Florida sky was so clear and blue, it hurt his eyes. The forest-green grass of the outfield cushioned his feet as he tracked fly balls. The infield dirt was so smooth and free of imperfections that it resembled brown glass from Gord's position in short right field.

The only sounds that reverberated through the empty stadium were the sharp crack of the bat, the smack of the ball into rawhide leather, and snippets of baseball talk that were washed away by the warm southern breezes.

Simply put, it was a perfect day for baseball.

Pre-game batting practice was always an exercise in organized chaos. The position players were divided into groups of three. Each group got five rounds of batting practice in the cage, and each round consisted of five swings per player.

The groups not in the cage took their positions in the field to either shag flies or take grounders, all while working on their footwork and positioning. One protective screen was set up behind second base to collect batted balls, and one was set up in front of first base to protect the team's one-bagger while he received throws from the other infielders.

Coaches were often positioned to the sides of the batting cage to hit ground balls to select fielders. At any time, four balls could be in play at once, so it was imperative for players to stay on their toes.

The keys to a successful batting practice session were speed, flow, and an accurate, authoritarian batting practice pitcher. The Lakeland Wildcats' batting practice pitcher, Tim Reid, fit that description perfectly and ensured that the first two criteria were followed.

Squat and barrel-chested, Reid was a retired police officer who, thirty years earlier, had been a minor league teammate of Tom Conrad's. His intense personality and no-nonsense approach to the game had earned Reid the moniker of "Badger" among Lakeland's players. Of course, no one dared speak Reid's nickname in his presence, as there were rumours that he had maimed his share of criminals during his drug-busting days. One such tale involved the Badger's lopping off a drug dealer's fingers with shears to extract information. A story like that had to be true.

Ironically, no one had ever heard Reid raise his voice in anger. If something pissed him off, Reid would shoot the offending party an icy glare to voice his displeasure. Invariably, the message was received, and the questionable behaviour ceased.

A few years ago, according to several reputable sources, a loudmouth rookie had told Reid to "Go fuck himself" when asked to do wind sprints after a game. The next day, the kid's locker was cleared out, and he was never heard from again. Some theorized that the rookie had been banished to an independent league team in some one-stoplight, Podunk town in rural Idaho. Others maintained that he was fish food off the Gulf Coast. Either way, no one had ever mouthed off to Reid and survived to tell the tale.

Besides his role as team disciplinarian, the Badger was an invaluable member of the staff for the way he conducted batting practice. Players did not walk or jog under Reid's eye. They ran. They ran to join their group at the plate, they ran to their positions in the field, and they ran to collect stray balls.

Each player got exactly five pitches per round. You did not wait for a grapefruit in your wheelhouse. You hit the ball where it was pitched or you missed a swing. Some players, Tyson Dante especially, tried to goad Reid into getting an extra pitch or two. A quick glare from the Badger was all that was required to shoot down such a request.

The players put up with Reid's hard-ass, old-school approach for two reasons: one, they were terrified of him; two, he was the greatest batting practice pitcher most had ever seen.

Reid had the uncanny ability to pepper seventy-mile-an-hour fastballs into the strike zone for hours on end. He never tired, his velocity never dipped, and it took him about twelve seconds to zip in five pitches. This breakneck pace meant there was no time to slack off on the field. Laziness was non-existent on Lakeland's roster.

Gord was bent over at the waist, resting a hand on each knee. Perspiration dripped off the front of his nose and dark sweat stains slowly enveloped the breadth of his light blue warm-up shirt.

Mercifully, one last line drive signalled the end of the forty-five-minute session. Gord and a fellow pitcher picked up the protective screen behind second base and started toward the storage shed beyond the left field bleachers. Coach Reid's gruff, nicotine-strained voice cut through the air.

"Mattis! Skip wants to see you."

Gord left his teammate to struggle with the cumbersome screen and hustled toward the first base dugout. Jogging by Reid, he asked, "What's this about?"

Reid hooked a thumb toward the dugout. "Don't know. He's in his office."

Tom Conrad sat in the manager's office with his feet propped up on the cheap metal desk. He was filling out that night's lineup card when Gord knocked on the open office door.

"You wanted to see me, Skip?"

Conrad, his wire-framed glasses perched at the tip of his nose, peered at Gord over the top of a thick binder crammed with paper. "Yes. Gord. Come in."

He motioned to an antiquated chair that sat in front of his desk. Gord, ignoring the torn fabric and mysterious stain that diagonally bisected the seat cushion, took a seat, and Conrad dived right in, straight to the point. "You know I've always been a fan of yours. A lot of these guys look at you like a big brother. It's your second year on the squad and you provide a viewpoint that the guys respond to: advice that's not from a coach."

Gord swallowed hard, knowing that qualifying criticism was sure to follow those kind words.

"That being said, your on-field performance hasn't been where I had hoped. Being my left-handed specialist, I know you haven't gotten a lot of work." Conrad shuffled through the papers on his desk. "Let's see: fifteen innings, 5.50 ERA,[1] twenty hits, two walks, and ten strikeouts. My biggest concern is your batting average against: .302." He raised his eyebrows, waiting for an explanation.

"I'm throwing strikes, but I'm catching too much of the plate. My arm feels good." Gord paused and looked Conrad straight in the eye. "Tom, I know I can turn this around."

Conrad met Gord's gaze and surveyed his oldest player for a

1 ERA = earned run average.

moment. "I think you can, too. And I'm going to give you every opportunity to do so. Here's the thing: as you know, we drafted seven pitchers in the June draft. Once we get them all signed, they'll be sent to the Gulf Coast League. Our top arms from rookie ball will be coming to Lakeland and we need spots for them. The front office has targeted a couple of our guys as 'make or break.' You're one of them."

Gord understood where Conrad was going with this speech. At twenty-four years old, he was ancient for A ball. The organization was basically giving him an ultimatum. Produce or take the train.

Conrad continued his monologue. "Starting tomorrow, I'm going to use you as my long guy out of the pen. Based on your conditioning, I know you can handle the increased workload. You have six weeks. If we see marked improvement in that time, I'll convince the front office to keep you. If not, then we'll have to . . ." His voice trailed off.

Conrad hated cutting players. Back in his hell-raising days, he never gave the process a second thought. Coherence wasn't a certainty with Conrad back then. Caring about the emotions of his players wasn't even on his radar.

Now, with his new-found faith, the process affected Conrad worse than the kids whose dreams he shattered. Most of the players he released had no backup plan: no education, no skills outside of their ability to play baseball. After cutting a player in his office, both parties would often emerge with tear-stained faces and red eyes.

Gord appreciated his manager's candour. "Thanks for being honest with me, Tom. And for the opportunity to prove myself to the organization. I won't let you down."

"I know you won't." Conrad smiled. "Okay, Gordie. Get back out there and get loose."

Walking back through the clubhouse, Gord encountered Danny Johnson hurriedly trying to tie his spikes and put his uniform on at the same time. Johnson squinted at Gord through bloodshot eyes. The smell emanating from his pores was a mixture of Jack Daniels and, knowing Danny's track record, unsatisfactory sex.

"Where did you end up last night?"

Danny grinned at Gord through the suffocating headache his Jack and Coke-induced hangover had provided. "I fucked a Mom last night. She was thirty-one, with two kids. She dropped me off at the park after she took her son to tennis camp. Unreal."

Gord looked at Danny with a mixture of shock and wonder. "How was she?"

"Amazing body; fake tits. You could tell she had a couple kids, though. It was like trying to fuck a parachute."

Gord winced at the mental image Danny had just created. "Conrad's in his office. He hasn't noticed you're late. Let's go toss before he does."

Gord situated himself on the right field foul line, approximately fifteen feet in front of the clay warning track surrounding the field. Danny stood across from Gord, perpendicular to the foul line. Capping the distance between them at one hundred feet, they started off with light tossing to warm up their arms and defuse any mechanical kinks that might crop up during the initial phase of their catch.

Their conversation meandered between Lakeland's chances against their opponents, the Sarasota Redbirds, and the more intricate details of Johnson's activities the previous night.

Apparently, Danny's lady friend was a waitress at Billy's Beach Bar and Grill in downtown Lakeland. A constant barrage of cheesy pickup lines and saccharine compliments, plus a steady diet of tequila shots at the end of her shift, had enabled Johnson to coerce the woman to take him back to her place. They were greeted at the door by her mother, who was pulling babysitting duty for her twice-divorced daughter.

Danny's moral ambiguity aside, it was hard not to admire his go-for-broke approach. The kid had brass balls and did not discriminate when it came to pursuits of the flesh. With his arm draped around the inebriated daughter, he bravely faced the enraged mother, on the downslope of middle age, and had the audacity to suggest a threesome.

Not surprisingly, the request was vehemently denied. But Johnson was somehow still able to sleep with the daughter and emerge with his scrotal possessions intact. Such is the life of a young professional athlete with a seven-figure bank account.

Their conversation eventually stopped completely, as Danny moved farther away from Gord to stretch out their arms. Now, the only sound between them was the whir of the ball as it smacked into the glove.

Gord threw with Danny most days, except when either was scheduled to pitch. Danny had the best arm on the team, and his long-toss capabilities were legendary amongst his Lakeland teammates. Most guys on the team were able to throw just under 300 feet with relative ease; some of the stronger arms reached significantly north of that distance with a parabolic arc and a crow hop. But Danny was on an entirely different level. He could throw 350 feet with minimal effort.

Without breaking a sweat, Danny reared back, took one step forward and unleashed a missile that exploded into Gord's glove 325 feet away.

Goofing around before batting practice one day, Danny stood at home plate at Mercantile Stadium and tried to throw a ball over the centre-field fence, 405 feet away. Putting everything he had into his magical right arm, Johnson let fly with a toss that defied logic. Jaws slacked throughout the park, as the ball disappeared over the centre-field wall and came to rest beside a Buick parked in the ancillary parking lot of the stadium. Danny could throw a ball farther than most Wildcats' infielders could hit one.

Gord loved the challenge of long toss with Danny. Gord himself could break the 300-foot barrier, but beyond that, his throws usually bounced and rolled to Danny at the other end of the field. Gord used the long-toss sessions to keep his arm strong and injury-free during the season.

The experience also forced Gord to acknowledge a sobering realization: he would never have the innate ability of a talent like Danny, so he had to compensate by working harder than his counterparts to ensure his survival in the cutthroat world of minor league baseball.

As their session drew to a close and Danny moved back to distances achievable by regular humans, Gord recalled a seminal moment in his career that also revolved around long toss. To him, it was his turning point in the game and, although he didn't know it at the time, it would ultimately fuel his development from a middling talent into a legitimate prospect. His thoughts took him back to Ann Arbor and the fall of 2000.

# September 2000

## Ann Arbor, Michigan
## Singer Park

The under-seventeen WABA travel team warmed up on the field at Singer Park before their last practice of the year. The team was scheduled to take part in a season-ending tournament in Albany, New York, that weekend. The tournament brought together some of the top travel teams in the Northeast and it was considered the crown jewel of the autumn baseball season.

The nucleus of the team was basically unchanged from previous years, although some new additions filled out the roster. The coaching staff was still intact, with Dave Kinsey at the helm and Michael Mattis as his second-in-command.

Gord, reassigned as a reliever, was relegated to mop-up duty on the pitching staff. He entered only games that were no longer in doubt, with his team either way ahead or way behind. Gord understood that some people were born with God-given, natural ability, and some weren't. He knew he was in that second group.

An example of a player with that natural talent was Reggie Gosselin, one of the aforementioned new additions. Gosselin, a pitcher from Myrtle Beach, South Carolina, had moved to Ann Arbor earlier in the summer with his family.

For a sixteen-year-old in Michigan, Reggie threw straight gas. During his first practice with Gord's team, the coaches clocked him at eighty-two miles per hour. That rose more than a few eyebrows around Ann Arbor minor baseball circles. From that point forward, Gosselin was the team's workhorse. Dave Kinsey ran him out to the mound every chance he could, at the expense of Gord and some of the team's other lesser lights.

Not surprisingly, Gosselin was the crown jewel of the team, and the coaching staff treated him as such. All players were required to show up ninety minutes before each game and were expected to attend all games, regardless of playing time. That meant Gord spent the majority of his summer vacation nailed to the right side of the unforgiving aluminum bench.

Of course, these rules did not apply to a prodigious talent like Reggie. He operated under terms similar to Roger Clemens's playing contract from the middle of the decade. Gosselin showed up only for the games he pitched and he always threw within a twenty-mile radius of Ann Arbor. There were no weary, soul-sapping road trips for Reggie the Rocket.

However, the special treatment didn't alienate Gosselin from the rest of the squad; he was a genuinely nice kid who was well-liked by his teammates, and such treatment of a star pitcher was fairly typical in the annals of organized baseball. Pitchers were considered a rare breed and were usually given more leeway—when it came to following team rules and regulations—than position players. As long as Gosselin kept stringing lines of zeroes together on the scoreboard every week, the coaching staff, to put it eloquently, didn't give a shit what he did when not on the mound.

Michael Mattis definitely took a shine to the young Gosselin. Gord assumed it was because Reggie had the talent he sorely lacked. Whatever the reason, Gord looked on with envy at the burgeoning baseball relationship between his father and his teammate.

As the practice wound down, and before Dave Kinsey could initiate the post-workout hell known as wind sprints, the team split into pairs for some long toss. Since there was an odd number of players on the team, a coach normally joined the fray to make things even. Much to Gord's chagrin, this long-toss session partnered Reggie with his dad.

Gord, a few pairs down from his father, was partnered with the team's fifth outfielder and his closest friend on the team, Andrew Montgomery. They bonded primarily over their lack of playing time and their jealousy of team stars like Jason Hamilton. Montgomery tried to initiate conversation, but the attempt fell on deaf ears as Gord's focus was glued to the interaction between his father and Reggie.

As each group increased their throwing distance, Gord heard a steady stream of superlatives emanating from his father's mouth. "What an arm!" "You're really throwing some smoke, Reggie."

"Christ, we're 200 feet away and he's still bringing it on a line." "He throws a heavy ball; it just explodes into the glove!" "To throw faster, you have to train the muscles to throw faster." "I wish more guys threw long toss to improve their arm strength—especially pitchers."

This last comment shot out the side of Michael's mouth. The words seared through Gord like a razor-sharp spear slicing through a sheaf of paper. The air whooshed out of his lungs and his shoulders sank in disappointment.

After the tournament in Albany, in which Gord pitched exactly two innings at the end of a 15–2 drubbing, Michael Mattis was still singing the praises of Gosselin's right arm at the end-of-season banquet. Before presenting the Cy Young Award—given to the top pitcher on the team—Michael delivered a flowery, overwrought speech telling the players and their parents what a pleasure it was having Gosselin on the team. He remarked that Gosselin "led by example and provided a blueprint to the rest of the staff on how to reach their potential on the mound."

Gord was hurt by his father's words. He wanted nothing more than to hear his dad speak so glowingly about *his* talents. Unfortunately, Gord knew such praise was unlikely to ever come.

The rest of the awards ceremony was a painstakingly boring affair for Gord—primarily because he was stapled to his seat while the trophies were given out. He had no chance of winning the most valuable player, top hitter, or top fielder awards. In fact, Gord couldn't even win the much-maligned most improved trophy, which was always given to a player who was terrible at the beginning of the year and just slightly turned down the suck by the time playoffs rolled around.

On the car ride home after the banquet, Gord sat in silence in the passenger seat, deep in thought. Growing up, he had always heard horror stories of young pitchers blowing out their arms due to overuse. Amateur baseball was littered with cautionary tales of torn rotator cuffs and shredded elbows from poor mechanics, throwing too many breaking balls, and throwing too many pitches in general.

There were only so many bullets in a pitcher's arm. Pitching was one of the most anatomically stressful activities in sports. Each time a pitcher threw, the arm wanted to fly out of the socket. The only mechanisms in place to prevent that from happening were the tendons and ligaments of the shoulder girdle.

Therefore, Gord had always been reticent to really let loose and throw as hard as he could. In fact, he babied his arm to an obsessive degree. He would throw only fastballs and changeups. To that point in his career, he had flatly refused to throw breaking balls.

Gord avoided heavy lifting with his left arm and shoulder whenever possible. He always carried his book bag on his right side and even brushed his teeth with his right hand to avoid unnecessary strain on his left arm.

His reluctance to use his pitching arm in non-baseball-related activities carried over to the realm of self-gratification as well. But, as he soon discovered, the use of his non-dominant hand was actually a blessing in disguise.

As Michael pulled into their driveway, Gord realized he was at a crossroads in his baseball career. What was the point of going to such lengths to preserve his arm when it didn't translate to success on the field? He had watched his peers—who threw breaking balls every other pitch and threw their fastballs as hard as they could—rocket past him in pitching talent and ability, while he languished at the bottom of the coaches' depth chart.

Sure, Gord wouldn't be able to play baseball at a higher level if he hurt his arm, but he sure as hell wasn't going anywhere with the way he pitched now. Seeing the way his father fawned over an arm like Gosselin made him think that throwing hard would be a way to make his dad proud.

Gord unbuckled his seat belt and looked at his father. "Hey, Dad, do you wanna throw some long toss?"

"Why?" Michael looked at his son dismissively. "What's the point? The season's over."

"Come on. It's still light out. I really want to throw."

Intrigued by his son's assertiveness, Michael agreed to the long toss session. They walked to a small parkette adjacent to the family bungalow. From the first toss, Gord threw like he had something to prove.

Instead of lightly floating balls into his father's mitt to warm up his arm, Gord peppered rockets into Michael's glove with a vengeance.

"Take it easy. You're going to hurt yourself."

"My arm feels fine. I can handle it."

Gord flicked his glove toward his father, indicating that he wanted Michael to move back, increasing the distance between them. Gord's audible grunts of exertion that followed each of his throws were surpassed only by the THWOCK of the ball into Michael's mitt.

Gord furrowed his brow in concentration as he geared up for another toss, a trail of perspiration sliding down his back.

Each throw was a purge of years of pent-up frustration for Gord: frustration at his lack of athletic ability, frustration from the taunts of his teammates, and frustration from the perceived disappointment of his father. A boiling rage fuelled every frozen rope he rifled to Michael.

Again and again, he launched the ball at his father with an animalistic ferocity. Finally, after fifteen long minutes, Gord, overcome with emotion and exhaustion, lobbed one last throw to his father, turned on a dime, and stalked back toward his house.

"Where are you going?" Michael inquired. "You were doing well." He jogged to catch up to his son.

"So, now you're talking to me, Dad. Am I one of your favourites on the team now because I showed you I can throw hard?"

"What do you mean? I don't have any favourites."

"Oh bullshit! I see how embarrassed you are when I pitch. How you wish I was more like Reggie."

"Reggie? What does this have to do with Reggie?"

"I see the way you drool all over him. How you always give him encouragement. You barely talk to me after I pitch. You just sit there with a pissed-off look on your face."

"I do not—"

"Give me a fucking break!"

Gord snatched the ball out of his father's glove, turned, and heaved it into the woods encircling the field. He took off at a run toward their house, entered, and slammed the front door in fury. Michael was left to stare wordlessly at the ball's final destination and contemplate the stinging words and new-found *cojones* of his only son.

# July 2008

## Lakeland, Florida
## Mercantile Stadium

The lacklustre game against the Sarasota Redbirds would have tested the patience of the most fanatical baseball enthusiast.

Sloppy play, defensive miscues, and numerous mental mistakes marred what should have been an entertaining contest between two of the Central Florida League's long-time rivals. As the moon muscled its way into the cloudless night sky, and the game began its third hour, the Redbirds and Wildcats were still mired in the bottom of the sixth.

With runners on first and second, Tyson Dante got a hold of a 3–1 fastball and crushed it into the left field gap, plating both runners. The double put Lakeland up by a field goal, 10–7.

Moments later, the bullpen phone jingled off its perch on the pen wall. Tim Reid, pulling double duty as the Wildcats' bullpen coach, answered the phone before the end of the first ring. He held the receiver to his ear, listened intently for a moment, and replaced the phone back in its cradle without speaking a word.

To describe the Badger as a man of few words was an understatement. During one of the more arduous bus trips after a game in early May, a bet was placed by some of the Wildcats looking to pass the time: How many words would Reid speak over the course of the four-hour trip? The winning guess, made by reliever Chris Seaboard, was eleven. Although that number didn't include the derivatives of "fuck" uttered by Reid after Danny Johnson accidentally spilled beer on him. Danny had been running up the aisle celebrating a complete game shutout, when he lost his balance and showered an unsuspecting Reid with a can of beer.

The multimillion-dollar contract paid by the front office and a lightning-quick intervention by Tom Conrad was the only reason Danny did not end up as roadkill on a desolate stretch of Florida freeway.

"Seaboard. Get loose," Reid growled, passing along Conrad's instructions.

Chris Seaboard jumped up and started stretching. The rest of the staff sat up a little straighter, knowing they could be called on at any point to enter the game.

Ordinarily, the denizens of the Wildcats' bullpen would be hard-pressed to know the score at that juncture in the game, especially if Danny was pitching. Say what you want about Danny's choice of extracurricular activities, the kid was definitely a workhorse and he ate up a lot of innings for Lakeland's beleaguered bullpen.

Typically, conversations in the bullpen touched on topics emblematic of twenty-something males with too much time on their hands. Not surprisingly, global economic policy and international diplomacy did not rank highly as talking points. Usually, the guys just tried to figure out which woman in the stands had the biggest tits. Or who got laid the night before. And that was pretty much it. Rinse and repeat.

Such scintillating banter was stifled today, as the implosion of Wildcats starter Chad Cole required every reliever to focus on an impending appearance. As the home half of the sixth inning came to a close, Seaboard jogged toward the mound to the strains of "Until It Sleeps" by Metallica.

Gord glanced down the bench, the dirt covered in a sea of dip spit and sunflower seed shells, and pondered the social hierarchy that had developed in the bullpen over the course of the young season.

Each reliever on the staff occupied a rung of varying height on the bullpen pecking order. This position, determined early in spring training, was the result of a number of factors: pitching ability, experience, personality, likeability, confidence, and gregariousness. Where a pitcher ended up on the social ladder was ultimately dependent on his ability to jell with his teammates. Those unable to do so found themselves cast down to the bottom rungs, basically ostracized by the rest of the staff.

Gord Mattis, as the elder statesman on the roster and a popular figure in the clubhouse, was close to the top tier of the hierarchy. Where he fell short was pitching ability; a situational lefty with a ho-hum fastball could not be the Alpha Dog of the bullpen.

And, while Gord had an easygoing demeanour off the field, once he stepped between the white lines, he was all business. His greatest pet peeve was people who didn't respect the game. He was the de facto judge of Lakeland's Kangaroo Court, fining players a handful of dollars each time they did something stupid or disrespectful on the field. Gord took it upon himself to admonish any player deemed to be in violation of baseball's unwritten code.

Gord policed opposing teams as well. He was always the first Wildcats pitcher to plunk an opponent who pimped a home run or committed a similar transgression. Gord considered playing professional baseball a privilege and he hated to see the game's integrity marred by questionable on-field behaviour.

This commitment to the honour of his profession rankled some of the team's younger players, who had a cavalier attitude toward the sport. Gord couldn't stand guys who coasted through games, took baseball for granted, and believed the game owed them something.

The undisputed Alpha Dog of the bullpen was Steve Anderson, a six-foot-five 240-pound behemoth from the University of Georgia. Drafted in the first round, after a sophomore year in which he averaged an astonishing fourteen strikeouts per nine innings, Anderson possessed a rising fastball that occasionally touched triple digits.

Unfortunately, Anderson didn't have another pitch. When you throw in the upper nineties in college, there's no need for secondary stuff. Anderson had little difficulty overpowering kids stressed out about term papers and finding gainful employment after graduation. Getting guys out whose sole purpose was to play baseball at the major league level posed more of a problem. He was used as the team's closer, but the organization projected him to be a top-of-the-rotation starter. Therefore, the Lakeland coaching staff had worked tirelessly with him to develop a more balanced arsenal.

"Mattis," Anderson asked, "can you show me your changeup grip again?"

To survive in A ball, Gord had to mix speeds and keep hitters off balance. Otherwise, teams would feast on his mediocre fastball and his career would be snuffed out like a wax candle on a deserted dinner table. For that reason, Gord, through necessity, possessed one of the better changeups on the staff.

"Yeah, throw me a ball," Gord replied.

Holding the ball loosely in his palm, with his thumb and forefinger making a circle on the side of the stitched leather, Gord lectured Anderson on the nuances of throwing a good changeup. He divulged how he sometimes varied the pressure on the ball with his fingertips to get more movement with the pitch. As Anderson listened attentively, Gord told his fellow pitcher to release the ball with a snap of the wrist, akin to pulling down a window shade.

Just as Gord was about to jump into a dissertation on the merits of gripping the ball parallel to the seams, as opposed to perpendicular, he was interrupted by Jeff Merkle. Merkle was one of the bottom rungs on the bullpen ladder.

"Hey, guys! Did you watch the highlights last night?"

"No, we didn—"

Gord was cut off by Merkle's incessant blather. "The web gems were unreal! Two sick diving catches. And St. Louis hit a walk-off grand slam in the tenth to beat Cincinnati. Has anyone seen that new Will Ferrell movie?"

Both Gord and Anderson looked at Merkle in dumbfounded amazement. The speed and inanity of the words that spewed from his mouth were simply astonishing. Silence was a foreign concept to Merkle. He deemed it necessary to fill any dead air with constant chatter about any pop culture topics currently occupying the public consciousness. That was one of the three reasons Merkle was cast down to the depths of the bullpen hierarchy. The second was that, quite simply, he sucked. He was a 45th-round draft pick. In the mid-1990s, a front-office executive from Chicago had drafted his daughter higher.

No one could quite understand why Merkle even had a roster spot. He had terrible off-speed pitches and mediocre control, and his fastball couldn't dent a pillow. Merkle was relegated strictly to mop-up duty in blowouts. Even in those no-pressure situations, he was somehow able to produce an earned run average over nine. There were rumours that Merkle had an uncle in the front office—that had to be the only explanation why his carcass was still occupying a spot on the staff.

The third and final reason why he was so unpopular among the other pitchers was that Merkle made Eddie Haskell look like Stanley Kowalski. He kissed so much ass to gain favour with the coaching staff that the team was surprised his nose wasn't permanently brown. Merkle volunteered for so many mundane clubhouse duties and was so eager to blindly agree to everything the coaching staff said, that the team derisively gave him the nickname "Rudy," after the character in the universally loved movie of the same name.

A story of inspiration and beating the odds, it was one of the few films deemed acceptable for males to show emotion and cry. Merkle thought the nickname was a term of endearment, which just encouraged his annoying behaviour.

"Will Ferrell is awesome. You guys really need to see it. It might be funnier than *Anchorman*; actually, maybe not *Anchorman*, but definitely better than *Blades of Glory*. There's this one scene when he—"

Anderson could not listen to any more. "Rudy, would you shut the fuck up? I don't give a shit. Five minutes of silence, please."

Completely lacking self-awareness, Merkle bounced up, moved to the other end of the bench and tried to engage two other members of the staff in the same pointless drivel. Mattis and Anderson looked at each other and just shook their heads, turning their attention back to the game, in case one of them was called upon.

After crossing the four-hour-and-thirty-minute threshold, the game finally ended on a walk-off bloop single by Tyson Dante in the bottom of the ninth. It was Dante's fifth hit of the night, tying the Lakeland team record.

The next afternoon, Gord was alone in the team's dank and dusty weight room, prepping for the rubber match against the same Sarasota Redbirds. The digital clock on the barren, paint-chipped wall read 2:00 p.m.

He climbed underneath a plate-ridden barbell to complete a set of heavy back squats. The first pitch wasn't scheduled until 7:30 p.m., so most players wouldn't stroll into the park for another two hours.

Gord found it therapeutic to train alone. Most players treated their strength training sessions as a glorified social hour, completing only a light set of work every five to ten minutes in between bouts of conversation.

The only things Gord needed to keep him company in the weight room were the driving beat of heavy metal rock music crackling through the primitive sound system, a pool of sweat dripping off his body, and gymnastics chalk streaked across his hands, wrists, and forearms.

Gord found it unbearable to watch the rest of the team train in such a haphazard manner. Their workouts lacked purpose and focused too much on what he termed "Venice Beach" muscles: chest and biceps. A high bench press or preacher curl had a very limited application to baseball. Those exercises lacked functionality and were basically useless in developing true total body strength and power.

The majority of the team put in only enough work to get the coaching staff off their backs. They preferred to spend their time working on baseball skills rather than hitting the weights. Gord was the opposite. He understood the benefits of heavy-weight, low-rep strength training and the positive effects it had on his pitching performance, stamina, and recovery.

Gord painfully finished the fifth rep of his 375-pound work set and carefully racked the weight. Out of the corner of his eye, he noticed movement near the entrance. Tom Conrad strode purposefully into the centre of the tiny weight room and switched off the music.

"Mattis, what are you doing here?"

"Just putting in my work, Skip," Gord replied in between heavy intakes of breath.

"Don't you remember our chat yesterday? You're my long guy. I want you to throw three innings tomorrow afternoon."

"I know, but I always lift heavy the day before I pitch. It helps me mentally prepare."

"Okay, if you say so. I would think you'd want to be fresh. This is a very important stretch coming up for you." Conrad considered Gord for a moment. "I do like how you're here early, though. It sets a good example for the younger guys."

Turning on his heel, Conrad ended the conversation and exited the weight room swiftly, closing the door behind him. Gord flicked the music back on and began unracking the bar. *Typical*, he thought. The questioning of his fanatical commitment to strength training was nothing new. Coaches and teammates had long doubted the effectiveness of such a training strategy, but Gord was undeterred in his devotion.

In Gord's mind, it was the thousands of hours he spent toiling in the gym that led to a career in professional baseball. Otherwise, the opportunity to play baseball for a living would have vanished into the air like the last wisps of smoke on a dying fire.

# April 2002

## Ann Arbor, Michigan
## Riverside Stadium

"Strike one!"
"Strike two!"
"Strike three!"

The Huron High River Rats closed out their third victory of the fledgling spring season with a close 3–1 decision over their Pioneer High School rivals. Gord Mattis, a senior and the team's star closer, shut down the Pioneers' offence in the bottom of the seventh, striking out the side on eleven pitches. All fastballs.

Huron High's catcher ran out to the mound and thrust his right hand toward Gord for a congratulatory shake. Gord, revelling in the admiration and backslaps from his teammates, looked into the crowd and noticed his father standing and clapping along with the rest of the Huron High parents.

The relationship between Gord and his father had marginally improved since their verbal blowup two years earlier. That fight was a watershed moment for them—they had never argued to that extent and ferocity before. The house was filled with the suffocating sounds of silence for weeks after their infamous long-toss confrontation, but the rift between Gord and Michael began to thaw shortly after the first snowfall of the year.

The thing that almost tore the Mattis men apart brought them back together: baseball.

Once father and son were back on speaking terms, Gord embarked, for the first time in his career, on a rigorous off-season long-toss and weight-training regimen. No longer wanting to be ridiculed by teammates for his lack of skill and ability, Gord completely devoted himself to the program designed by Michael.

All of the insults and taunts Gord received throughout his career were fuel for each workout session. He saw the faces of his tormentors every time he wanted to quit. Every ounce of sweat, every weight lifted, and every throw was a gigantic "fuck you!" to all who had written him off as a below-average talent who only made teams because of nepotism.

The indoor baseball facility where they played long toss became a second home to Gord and Michael. They spent many long, lonely winter nights in the vast space, slinging baseballs back and forth to each other.

As the harshness of winter gave way to the hopefulness of spring, Gord finally found himself with the body of an athlete. With 185 pounds tightly packed onto a six-foot frame, both father and son were excited to see how their hard work would transfer to the baseball field.

The results were extraordinary.

By the end of his junior season, Gord had moved from a roster afterthought to Huron High's top relief pitcher. His fastball steamed past respectability and regularly sat in the low eighties. Huron High's coaching staff still didn't trust him to carry a starter's workload, but Gord didn't mind.

He loved the adrenaline rush of closing. He relished the responsibility of having the team depend on his arm to finish off victories. It was a far cry from the complete lack of confidence that had previously defined his career.

The highlight of Gord's junior year, and probably his life at that point, came in the sectional playdowns. Huron High was pitted against a powerhouse school from Flint. The River Rats clung to a tenuous 5–4 lead heading into the bottom of the seventh when Gord was called in from the bullpen.

A leadoff single, sacrifice bunt, fly out, and walk had runners on first and second, with two out and Flint's cleanup hitter striding to the plate. A deep pit of despair formed in Gord's gut as he watched the batter ready himself in the box. The slugger was someone from Gord's baseball past; a vestigial reminder of all the disappointment he had felt at the hands of the game he loved.

Jason Hamilton grinned out at Gord from the batter's box. The Hamilton family had moved to Flint eighteen months earlier, but the change in scenery did little to quell Jason's extraordinary talent.

Hamilton led the state in RBIs[2] and was fifth in home runs. The move also didn't change the fact Hamilton was still an asshole.

Hamilton hocked a glob of spit toward the mound and mouthed the words, "You're fucking dead," to a visibly shaken Gord.

Gord, his confidence dropping, stepped off the mound and wiped his brow with the back of his left hand. *How do I pitch to him?* As visions of a Hamilton walk-off home run swirled around in his head, Gord realized two things:

First, Jason Hamilton hadn't seen him pitch in over two years. To Jason, Gord was still the doughy coach's son with no semblance of talent. He had no idea of the work Gord had put in over the off-season to transform himself into a bona fide closer. *He's expecting me to throw slop at him, if I get it near the plate at all*, Gord reasoned.

Second, Gord could use Jason's massive ego to his advantage. It was obvious that there was no doubt in Jason's mind that he was going to break Gord's heart and win the game for his team. Jason didn't want to just get on base. He wanted to deposit Gord's offering about 400 feet away in left centre. He looked way too comfortable standing in the batter's box. Gord decided to shake him up a bit; make him move his feet.

There was only one way to do that.

Gord took the sign from his catcher, reared back, and let fly with the hardest fastball he could muster. The ball shot toward Jason's jugular vein, forcing him to pirouette wildly out of the way of the incoming heat seeker.

Jason, chest heaving, stared incredulously at Gord, shocked at the velocity of the pitch. He quickly regained his composure and once again readied himself in the box. However, this time his feet weren't quite so steady. There was an imperceptible shift in his balance, which marked his unease.

Gord smiled inwardly. His ploy had worked. Jason's focus was not entirely on hitting. He was now concerned about taking a pitch in the chops.

Gord took the sign and steamed in another inside fastball, but this one caught the edge of the plate, which froze a flinching Jason. The count was even: one ball, one strike.

---

2 RBIs– runs batted in.

Huron High's catcher flashed the sign for a changeup, but Gord shook him off emphatically. *He's looking change, let's stick with the heat.*

Gord came set, checked the runners, and sent another fastball screaming over the outer half. Once again, Jason watched it go by. He was looking for the local and got the express. 1–2.

The count in his favour, Gord didn't want to fool around with a waste pitch. He wanted to wipe that smug smile off Jason Hamilton's face right then and there. The River Rat's catcher signalled for another off-speed pitch, and once again, Gord shook him off.

The catcher, suddenly cognizant of what Gord was trying to do, threw down his index finger. It was the universal signal for the old number one. But this time, he swirled his finger around in a circular motion as if to say, *throw it harder than before.*

Gord took a step off the mound and inhaled deeply. He was completely focused, drowning out the sound of the swelling crowd and the atmosphere around him. He shook his left arm vigourously, readying himself for the next pitch.

Completely ignoring the runners and lifting his right leg high, Gord ripped a fastball down the cock—right over the heart of the plate. The ball barreled toward home, just above Hamilton's belt buckle. Hamilton had started his swing early, but the ball got on him too quickly. His bat sailed beneath the ball, which smacked into the catcher's mitt with the sweetest sound Gord had ever heard.

Strrrriiiiikkkkkkke three! Game over.

Gord pumped his fist and was immediately swallowed into a victory huddle with the rest of his jubilant teammates. He was so caught up in the commotion that he didn't notice Jason Hamilton, ever the sportsman, fling his bat in disgust and stalk dejectedly back to the dugout, embarrassed by his former teammate and favourite target of ridicule.

Against Pioneer High, Gord's rather predictable pitch selection was typical of his senior season. Ever since he had shoved those bullets up Jason Hamilton's ass the previous year, he had fallen in love with the fastball.

Part of Gord's infatuation with throwing hard stemmed from this being the first time in his career that he actually possessed a pitch that caught batters' attention. He loved standing on the mound, with his one-weapon arsenal, basically daring the opposition to hit his preeminent pitch.

The results were there, as Gord's gaudy strikeout total could attest, but he had unintentionally turned himself into a thrower, not a pitcher. His fascination with the fastball led his off-speed repertoire to become severely atrophied and his mechanics to become a poorly timed mess. Gord was completely unable to replicate a consistent delivery.

Basically, his game plan was to enter the game for one inning and just throw as hard as he could until three outs were made. Gord's inconsistent mechanics led to significant control problems, but he was what baseball men deemed "effectively wild." Opponents rarely had their feet set against him: they were always wary of an errant fastball leaving stitch marks on their backsides.

If Gord didn't know where his pitches were going most of the time, what chance did the batters have?

Neither Huron High's coaching staff, nor Gord, were particularly concerned with his periodic bouts of wildness, or his inability to throw an off-speed pitch. The coaches were just happy to win ball games, and Gord was thrilled with his status as the team's star closer. If it ain't broke, don't fix it.

However, unbeknownst to Gord, his wildness and reliance on the fastball was actually detrimental to his development as a pitcher. While his "one-trick pony show" worked fine at the high school level, college ball diamonds were littered with guys who could throw hard, and much harder than he. College hitters feasted on fastball pitchers with no control. They just waited for a pitch in their wheelhouse and teed off like Tiger Woods during a range session.

None of this mattered much to Gord. He revelled in his ability to be a thrower who chucked gas. He was happier than he had ever been, finally a success at the game he loved. He saw no reason why all of his hard work and determination wouldn't propel him to a starring role at the post-secondary level as well.

But sometimes things don't always work out as they should. Gord's college career would personify that fact. Both on and off the field.

# July 2008

## Vero Beach, Florida

The dream was always the same.

> *Again and again, Gord's pitches fly all over the park—some falling short, some going too long, others thrown halfway up the baselines. None come close to the strike zone.*
>
> *He's powerless to stop it. The crowd's taunts become more derisive and vitriolic. The boos thunder down onto the field and rattle his eardrums.*
>
> *The walks and runs pile up like stacks of cordwood. Gord looks in desperation to the bullpen, longing for relief and an end to the nightmare, but no one is there. He is completely and utterly alone . . .*

The dream intruded on Gord's precious REM cycle, in advance of his pitching performances, like some sort of perverse Pavlovian response. Wiping the crusty sleep remnants out of his eyes, Gord shifted anxiously under the motel room's paper-thin sheets. They stank of disinfectant and watered-down detergent.

Staring at the ceiling, Gord realized he still had two hours before the shrill sound of the alarm clock would summon him to the ballpark. That afternoon, he was scheduled to pitch three innings against the Vero Beach Diablos in the first outing of his six-week organizational "tryout" created by Tom Conrad and the higher-ups in the front office. This truly was make-or-break time for his baseball career.

On the days he pitched, Gord's cheery demeanour and personable attitude were replaced with the steely gaze of a gladiator ready to do battle in the Coliseum. When he was scheduled to stand on the bump, his teammates knew it was best not to engage him in typical clubhouse chatter.

On the bus ride to the ballpark, the majority of the team congregated at the back of the bus away from the attentive ears of the coaching staff. Gord chose a row near the front, an empty seat beside him, and gazed out the window as his mind cleared and focused on the task at hand. Tunnel vision.

Approximately ninety minutes before the first pitch, the rest of the Wildcats were in various stages of undress in the clubhouse. Gord sat quietly at his locker, already in full warm-up gear. He gently rocked back and forth. The adrenaline charging through his body made it impossible to sit still.

Rap music blared through the clubhouse speakers, and quick bursts of conversation could be heard around the room as Lakeland readied itself for a tough game against the Diablos.

"Where are my spikes?"

"Do you have any dip? No, not regular. I like grape."

"My fucking glove just ripped."

"Dude, she was a pig. Stop nailing slumpbusters."

"Anyone have some pine tar?"

"Where's the clubhouse kid? I need new laces."

"Off-day tomorrow? I am getting so fucked up tonight."

"You're a cocksucker."

The music and conversation coalesced into ambient white noise to Gord. He waited patiently for one of his teammates to finish dressing so he could hit the field to warm up. Gord's regular throwing partner, on the days he pitched, was backup catcher Aaron Carmack.

Across the room, Carmack finished tying his laces, grabbed his catcher's mitt, and made his way toward the field entrance. Gord gave him a quick nod, motioned for him to get a ball, and followed him to the field.

Carmack, a tall, lanky redhead from Reno, Nevada, was basically the Bizzaro Jeff Merkle. He was extremely quiet and shy, and usually only spoke when spoken to. That's why Gord loved warming up with him before an outing. Gord didn't want to take part in any extraneous banter.

Stretching back to a comfortable distance in the outfield, Gord threw until a thick pool of sweat engulfed his body, and his arm felt ready to handle the rigours of throwing off a mound. Gord jogged toward Carmack, stationed along the left field foul line, and flipped him the ball.

"Thanks, Aaron."

Those were the first two words Gord had spoken since getting on the team bus that morning. He continued on to the clubhouse to change his undershirt and put on his jersey.

Scheduled to throw innings five through seven, Gord decided to take up residence in the dugout for the first part of the game, instead of his usual spot in the outfield bullpen.

Tom Conrad addressed his charges from the top step of the dugout. "Okay, fellas, let's work the count. Remember the signs. Good fundamental baseball. Let's get 'em."

A harmonious explosion of baseball chatter sprang to life in Lakeland's dugout as the Wildcats' leadoff hitter, Tristan Beem, strode to the plate.

"Hum babe!"

"Come on now, kid!"

"Here we go!"

"Start it off!"

"Atta boy!"

"Hey TB, have a day, kid!"

"Stay hot!"

Gord smiled. This unrestrained, juvenile exuberance was nonexistent in the bullpen. Baseball talk, no matter how nonsensical, was used primarily to keep players' heads in the game.

Pitchers didn't need to resort to baseball chatter to stay involved in the game. They always knew, well in advance, if they were scheduled to throw that day. Position players didn't have that luxury, as they could be called upon at any time to pinch hit, pinch run, or enter the game as a defensive replacement.

As a group, all pitchers were mentally fragile. Smart coaches knew they couldn't spring an appearance on a guy without advance warning, unless they wanted a pitcher with shaken confidence to take the hill. Like field goal kickers and hockey goalies, pitchers were delicate flowers and they had to be handled accordingly.

Gord watched Beem lace a single up the middle, and the bench erupted to life once again.

"Hey, babe!"

"There we go, there we go!"

"All day, boys, all day!"

"Keep the train moving!"

Batting second, Tyson Dante uncharacteristically lunged at the first pitch, popping it up directly behind home plate. The Diablos' catcher circled under it, tossed his mask in the opposite direction, and snared the ball with two hands. One away.

Dante smashed his bat onto home plate and stomped back to the dugout. His teammates gave him a wide berth and avoided eye contact. Dante slammed his bat and helmet into one of the dugout cubbyholes. Muttering and shaking his head, Dante crunched across the discarded sunflower seed shells and expectorated tobacco juice blanketing the dugout floor. He stopped suddenly when he spotted Gord gazing out onto the field.

"What the fuck are you doing in here?"

Gord, unaware Dante was referring to him, remained silent.

Dante walked up beside him and poked Gord in the left shoulder. "Gord! Why aren't you in the fucking bullpen?"

Gord shifted away from Dante's touch. He stared at the fiery third baseman like Dante had just ripped a huge fart in a closed elevator.

"What's your problem, Tyson?"

"You never sit on the bench; it fucking messed me up. That's why I popped out."

Gord looked at Dante with a look of stupefied amazement. "Jesus Christ," he muttered. He hopped off the bench and walked into the dugout tunnel to get away from Dante's superstitious idiocy. As he departed, he could hear Dante explaining to a nearby teammate how his at-bat was ruined by Gord's appearance in the dugout.

In the bottom of the fourth, Vero Beach, already in possession of a 5–1 lead, threatened with two on and two out. Gord, warming up in the bullpen, kept one eye on the field.

He knew his entrance into the game was imminent. Conrad wouldn't want the game to get much further out of reach. Sure enough, time was called, and Lakeland's manager emerged from his dugout perch and slowly walked to the mound. Conrad extended his left arm perpendicular to the ground and tapped the elbow with his right hand, signalling Gord into the game.

Gord flicked his glove toward the bullpen catcher. He always ended every bullpen session with the same pitch: a fastball right down the chute. Call it tradition or superstition, but Gord didn't feel comfortable unless his last warm-up pitch was a fastball that he tried to throw through the catcher's chest.

Gord walked through the creaky wooden gate separating the bullpen from the field. Taking a quick breath to steel himself, he jogged across the green expanse to meet his manager on the mound.

"Okay, Gordie, I need you to put this fire out before things get out of hand."

Gord, unblinking, nodded his head.

"Get us back on the sticks." Conrad's voice dropped to a whisper. "Remember, this is your time now. Make the most of it." With that, he patted Gord on the back and trudged toward the dugout with his hands tucked in his back pockets.

Gord stuck his glove under his arm and kneaded the ball between his hands. Dave Rockwood, Lakeland's catcher, covered his mouth with his mitt to dissuade the Diablos from trying to lip-read their conversation.

"One fast, two curve, three change?"

"Yep," Gord replied.

On the field, all baseball players engaged in the ridiculous act of covering their mouths when conversing, as though, in addition to tremendous baseball talent, opponents also had the ability to lip-read from one hundred feet away. It was ludicrous to think teams could acquire intricate knowledge of the opposition through such reconnaissance, but it was just one of the quirks that made the game so great.

Gord completed his eight warm-up pitches, and the umpire signalled for play to resume. Rockwood called for an outside fastball. Gord nodded, came set, checked the runners, and painted the black with a tailing two-seam fastball.

Rockwood moved to the inside corner and requested a curveball. He placed his glove at the batter's ankles, indicating he wanted the next pitch to finish low in the zone.

Gord's offering floated lazily to the plate with a modicum of break. The pitch sailed high for ball one. He slapped his thigh in disgust—a mental reminder to stay on top of the ball and finish his delivery with a violent Tomahawk chop.

Rockwood, in addition to being a physical freak with both power and speed, possessed a high baseball IQ. Pitchers loved the way he called a game. After the desultory results of the last pitch, Rockwood figured the batter would not expect another curve, so that is exactly what he called.

Gord, impressed with his catcher's confidence in his stuff, nodded in agreement. This time he unfurled a sharp curve with a sliding 10 o'clock to 4 o'clock break. The batter was caught way off balance and his bat flailed through the hitting zone. He managed to catch a small piece of Gord's offering and sent a meek grounder foul toward third base.

With the count at one ball and two strikes, Gord and Rockwood had a variety of options at their disposal. They could waste a pitch and get the batter to chase some more slow stuff low and away, or bust him inside with a fastball to back him off the plate. Then, with the count at 2–2, they'd have him set up for a circle change diving to the outer half.

But the Wildcats' battery decided to change the batter's eye level. After an off-speed pitch down in the zone, they silently agreed that a fastball at the letters would look too enticing to ignore. This would hopefully force the batter to either miss completely or pop out.

The runners danced off their bases, trying to take Gord's focus away from the man at bat. Gord came set and let fly. His pitch streaked toward the middle of the plate, but it was not at the letters as Rockwood's glove directed. This fastball was belt high.

The batter's eyes lit up as he recognized the missed location. He whipped his bat through the zone and made contact with the meat of the barrel, his arms fully extended.

Gord groaned audibly when he heard the perfect harmony of bat on ball. A pitcher like Danny Johnson or Steve Anderson would have been able to get away with a mistake pitch like that because they threw so hard. Gord Mattis didn't have that luxury.

The ball shot toward centrefield and the runners took off around the bases. With two outs, they were running on contact. Centrefielder Tristan Beem got an excellent jump and raced toward the warning track, hoping to catch up with the frozen rope.

The ball never got more than fifteen feet off the ground. Just as it began its downward arc, destined to collide with the base of the outfield wall, Beem, in full stride, leapt out and snared the ball in the webbing of his black mitt. His momentum pitched him forward and he crashed headlong into the protective padding of the fence. Dizzy, but unhurt, he thrust his glove into the air to show the entire stadium the inning's third out.

Gord smacked his bare hand and glove together, grateful for his centrefielder's great play. Hopping down the dugout steps, Gord bumped fists with his teammates and got a congratulatory pat on the ass from his manager for ending the Diablos' offensive threat.

He found Beem at the other end of the bench and slapped him on the back. "Thanks for saving my ass, TB. Great catch."

In the shower after the game, Gord reflected on his performance. *Not bad,* he thought. *It was a decent showing for my first outing as the long man out of the bullpen, but I need to be better. I'm still too inconsistent.*

Letting the hot water stream over his body, Gord went over his pitching line in his head: 3.1IP, 5H, 1BB, 2ER, 2K.[3] Lakeland had attempted a late comeback, which would have put Gord in line for the win, but they ultimately fell short 7–5.

"Gordo?" Steve Anderson poked his head into the shower.

"Yeah?"

"Hurry up and get dressed. We're going out for a few pops."

Gord shut off the shower and grabbed his towel. The lukewarm water pooled around his sandals, searching for the drain. He figured he could use a couple of beers to take the edge off.

"Give me ten minutes."

A group of Wildcats occupied a back table filled with pitchers of ice-cold beer and piping-hot wings, on the patio of Jack's Restaurant and Lounge. Overlooking the Atlantic on Ocean Drive, Jack's was a great place for the guys to relax in relative anonymity. About a mile

3 IP = innings pitched, H = hits, BB = walks, ER = earned runs, K = strikeouts.

north of the Riocan Country Club, the bar catered to upscale clientele looking for a middle-class experience.

Joining Gord and Anderson were Danny Johnson, Chris Seaboard, and JR Coltrane, a starting pitcher from Thousand Oaks, California. The conversation stuck to baseball while the guys ate, but, as the food cleared and the pitchers of beer sank to dangerously low levels—only to be replenished by their increasingly attractive waitress—they began to take notice of some of the female "talent" at the surrounding tables.

"Oh shit, look at that one." Johnson nodded toward the entrance.

A raven-haired beauty swivelled her shapely hips across the patio toward their table. She wore a tiny pair of denim jean shorts that would have made Daisy Duke blush. The shorts were perched atop a statuesque pair of silky smooth, olive-skinned legs. Upstairs, she wore a dangerously tight yellow spaghetti strap shirt, which barely concealed her bountiful breasts. Her cup literally runneth over.

Danny stared at Miss Duke with his mouth agape: the rest of the guys used a bit more discretion, but there was no denying that she was absolutely gorgeous. She also knew exactly what she was doing. An alluring smile pasted to her face, Miss Duke confidently strutted past the Wildcats and joined her two friends, also possessing qualities desired by the shallow male, at a nearby table.

Anderson whistled and shook his head. "A broad like that will get you in all kinds of trouble."

Prying their gazes away from the three Sirens, the guys embarked on a time-honoured tradition and rite of male bonding: the trading of sex stories. However, the stories quickly became a juvenile game of one-upmanship similar to fishermen telling tales of fish caught. "I swear to God, it was this big!"

Johnson was the only Wildcat not participating in the discussion. Not that he didn't have any stories, but he was completely transfixed by Miss Duke and her friends.

"Jesus, Danny, at least blink. She'll think you're a serial killer," Gord quipped to his roommate.

"I love this chick," Danny replied hungrily.

At that moment, the three ladies got up, checked to make sure every pair of male eyes had homed in on them, and strode into the bar.

Seaboard leaned across the table and smacked Danny in the shoulder. "Hey, Bonus Baby, you're going to have to bring out your wallet to seal this deal."

"You sure you can handle this, Danny Boy?" Coltrane inquired sarcastically.

"Fuck you, guys, I'm going in." With that, Danny jumped up from his seat and bounded into the bar.

Gord shook his head and smiled. "The kid's got balls, I'll give him that."

Fifteen minutes later, the patio door burst open and Danny stepped across the threshold with a megawatt grin stapled to his face. Miss Duke and her gal pals trailed close behind like he was the Pied Piper leading rats to the river.

The guys exchanged astonished glances, impressed at the game of their brash teammate. Danny and his new friends joined the Wildcats at their table. The sequence of events became clear when their waitress emerged onto the patio, carrying a tray full of shots and set it down in front of the group.

Danny whipped out his credit card in an elaborate gesture and handed it to the waitress. The display of plastic and copious amount of drinks was not lost on the ladies. They had found their meal ticket for the night.

Danny passed out seven shots, keeping one for himself. This barely made a dent in the tray. Things were going to get messy.

"What is this, tequila?" asked Coltrane.

"Yeah, buddy. Patron." Danny shot a look to the ladies. "Only the good stuff."

As the group brought the shots to their lips, Gord wavered. "Shit. I can't do tequila anymore. It wrecked me in college."

Danny admonished him. "Come on, Gordo, don't be a pussy. This isn't your college bullshit tequila; it goes down smooth."

"Yeah, that's what I'm worried about."

Miss Duke, privy to the conversation from her spot across from Gord, unsteadily rose out of her chair and leaned suggestively over the table. She flashed Gord her most devastating smile.

"Oh, just have some shots with us. We're lots of fun."

Her chest was directly at Gord's eye level. He considered her for a moment, studying the intricate details of her yellow shirt. He looked at Anderson to his left.

"How can I say no to that face?" he said with a conceding shrug.

Gord slammed the shot down his throat and signalled Danny to give him another.

The last time Gord got blindsided by tequila was during his freshman year at university. It was the night he was introduced to the wonderful world of collegiate binge drinking.

# September 2002

## University of Michigan

"Rooks!" Brent McPhee bellowed with the authoritative air of a drill sergeant. "Line up for your haircuts!"

McPhee was a senior and the captain of the University of Michigan Wolverines baseball team.

The ten rookies on the Wolverines' roster dutifully tried to organize themselves into a reasonable facsimile of a straight line. However, the three previous hours of drinking somewhat hindered their ability to think and move coherently.

The annual rookie night was the pre-eminent event on the baseball team's social calendar. Taking place the first weekend after team tryouts, it was an opportunity for the rookies and veterans to bond in a non-baseball setting. The event did wonders for team chemistry, and the mild hazing was a great way to introduce the first-year players to the traditions of Michigan baseball. The night also served notice to the freshmen on scholarships that no matter how good they were in high school, they were still lowly college rookies.

The Michigan baseball rookie night was much different from the reprehensible hazing rituals that caused a North American media maelstrom every time such activities were made public. Hazing customs that employed forced nudity, degradation, and sodomy with inanimate objects were the bailiwick of a few troubled athletes probably trying to cover up their own repressed feelings of latent homosexuality. Unfortunately, those disgusting and inappropriate rituals gave the fun, harmless hazing used by the baseball team a bad rap.

The team used the following games and activities to haze their rookies, all of which required the consumption of alcohol: Flip Cup, Beer Pong, Boat Races, and baseball trivia.

Each rookie was "owned" by a veteran who forced his protégé to don a ridiculous costume and then shaved his head into an entertaining and embarrassing pattern. Every year, without fail, the "Friar Tuck" was the most popular hairstyle.

A premium was put on fun for the rookies, but the team also made sure everyone was safe as well. The team captain stayed sober to transport drunken rookies back to their dorms. These deliveries were adventures unto themselves and had caused many disapproving looks from resident advisers over the years.

If a rookie puked, he was cut off and taken home. There were two awards for the night: First Rookie Down and Last Rookie Standing. Obviously, all rookies aspired to be in the latter category.

"Gentlemen, start your trimmers," Brent McPhee instructed his fellow veterans. He did a quick count of the wobbling first-year players. "Hold on, we're missing someone."

Matt Carbone, Michigan's first string catcher, entered the room. "I can't find Mattis. He ran off after I tried to get him to do a shot. He's pretty wasted."

"I think I saw him go upstairs with one of the softball chicks," offered left fielder John Sukrage.

The team held rookie night in conjunction with the women's softball team. The official story was that, with the common thread of baseball, it was beneficial to build camaraderie and support among the two programs. But in fact, as any male would agree, it was always more fun to drink and carouse when women were around.

"Shit, I don't want anyone going upstairs to the bedrooms," McPhee muttered. "Come on, Matty," he motioned to Carbone. "Boys, we'll be back in a minute."

As team captain, McPhee had offered his house, a three-storey Victorian with a huge backyard, as the location for the party. It was a great spot and it provided ample room for both teams to conduct their rookie nights comfortably.

The softball team was currently outside with the keg waiting for the guys to finish the haircuts. McPhee and Carbone hustled up the stairs to look for Gord.

At the end of the second-floor hallway, McPhee noticed that his door was ajar and the light was on. "If that fucker puked in my bed, I'll kill him."

Upon entering the room, both McPhee and Carbone erupted in laughter. Gord was flat on his back, shirtless, and completely passed out. A softball rookie was draped across his chest, also passed out, with her shirt around her neck. Their bodies were perpendicular to one another like some type of sacrilegious cross.

Still laughing, McPhee went to his window and shouted down to the softball team captain. "Hey Michelle, come here for a second. One of your girls needs some, uh, help."

The three of them were able to bring the girl back from her alcohol-induced haze rather quickly, but Gord was a bit more problematic. Once Michelle had her rookie out of the room and down the stairs, Carbone was able to rouse Gord out of his stupor with a few slaps to the head.

"Ohhhhhhhh, what do—what do you guys want?" Gord moaned.

"Time to get up, Sunshine, breakfast is ready," McPhee sarcastically replied.

"No, no, just—just let me stay here."

"Can't do it, pal. Because if you puke in my room, then I'll have to send you home in a body bag. Your family wouldn't like that very much. At least not until after midterms."

McPhee and Carbone got Gord to his feet and helped him navigate the stairs to join the rest of the team. Sukrage handed Gord a shot of tequila as a penalty for going AWOL. Gord, glassy-eyed, downed it with a flourish. As soon as the alcohol reached his stomach, Gord's eyes became large and his skin took on a greenish hue.

"I'mmmmmm gonnnnaaaaaa puke," he cried.

Searching for an exit, Gord lunged for the front door. He leaned over the porch railing and let fly with a consistent stream of vomit that lasted for the better part of a minute. The putrid stench wafted into his nostrils, making his eyes water. He slumped against the dilapidated railing, terrified any sudden movement would catalyze another expulsion from his system.

McPhee gestured to the rest of the baseball team, who stood in a semicircle on the porch watching their fallen comrade. "Gentlemen, we have our First Rookie Down!"

The other players broke out into applause and clapped the newly anointed rookie on the back.

"Nice job, rook," McPhee remarked to an oblivious Gord.

The wretched taste of bile pitched Gord over the railing once more.

"Jesus, I hope he pitches as well as he pukes," Carbone quipped.

Although Gord's senior season at Huron High had been terrific, he didn't possess the necessary stuff to be a scholarship athlete. And while he had received decent grades in high school, an academic scholarship was also out of the picture.

Gord, with his father's guidance, of course, decided to enroll at the University of Michigan to take advantage of the school's low tuition costs for in-state residents. Plus, UM had a terrific baseball program and a coach, Perry Picard, who encouraged walk-on players.

On freshman move-in day, Gord's heart was in his throat. While the campus was only a forty-five minute drive from the Mattis home, university would undoubtedly be a life-changing experience. Gord was leaving his father as a boy and would return a man.

His eyes were opened wide to a plethora of possibilities during the bedlam that was frosh week. For the first time in his life, he felt the seductive glances of girls wash over him. Gone were the outdated glasses that had defined Gord's high school days. He was now a desirable commodity among the fairer sex. It was a feeling he relished, as it had happened far too infrequently during his adolescence.

Unfortunately, baseball team tryouts coincided with the majority of frosh week activities, but Gord didn't mind. The college social scene could wait. He wanted to make the University of Michigan varsity baseball team more than anything in the world.

Gord's tryout got off to an inauspicious start. All prospective pitchers were required to get six outs in their first appearance: three against a team of other tryout players and three against a team comprised of returning Wolverines. This was how the coaching staff decided to weed through the walk-on dreamers and separate the wheat from the chaff.

Prior to his turn on the hill, Gord felt cautiously optimistic about his chances. He was one of three southpaws in camp and he was brimming with confidence after his successful high school senior season. Taking the mound to face the walk-on team, Gord felt the eyes of the coaching staff following his every move.

He toed the rubber, got the signal for a fastball, and threw it as hard as he could. It was a classic overthrow. The ball took off out of his hand and sailed above the unsuspecting catcher's head. Gord's offering crashed into the chain link fence behind home plate, and the resulting vibrations reverberated around the field.

The pitch didn't impress the coaches. They figured Gord was just another kid with limited baseball experience trying out for the team on a lark.

However, more important, it scared the living shit out of the batter and his teammates. All they saw was some freshman no one had ever heard of, with some decent giddy-up on his fastball, and no idea where it was going.

Gord was aware of the mood shift on the opposing bench and realized he could use his wildness to his advantage, as he had in high school. Sure enough, not one player on the tryout squad was eager to dig in against him. They all had "happy" feet. Although it took him fifteen pitches, Gord was able to strike out the side without a batter reaching base.

Now the coaching staff was intrigued. A lefty who could throw the ball in the low to mid-eighties was a valuable commodity on a college pitching staff.

The team of Wolverines, after witnessing Gord's performance, was eager to find out if the kid was for real. Gord, blissfully ignorant of the Wolverine hitters, decided to just attack them as though they were members of the tryout squad.

Throwing free and easy, Gord set down the first two hitters on strikes. At this point, the coaches were trying to figure out why they hadn't heard of him before. Coach Picard had visions of a left-handed starter dancing in his head.

Gord's final hitter was third baseman Brent McPhee, who had injected himself into the lineup because he wanted to see the freshman first hand. McPhee worked the count full. Ordinarily, Gord would automatically fire a fastball, not wanting to risk a walk. However, he knew McPhee was sitting dead red—just waiting for the heat.

Gord's performance thus far made him just cocky enough to try the curveball he had spent far too little time in high school trying to master. Gord figured he was playing with house money at this point anyway, so why not try to surprise the veteran?

Gord snapped off a 12 to 6 curveball that would have made Sandy Koufax blush. To say McPhee was caught off guard would have been an egregious understatement. His legs buckled faster than a newborn fawn trying to take its first steps.

Rung up on strikes, McPhee incredulously whipped his head

around to an equally surprised Gord, as if to say, "Where did that come from?" Walking back to the bench, the Wolverines' captain caught the eye of his head coach and gave him a nod. Picard nodded back. Six batters, six strikeouts. Gord had made the team.

Even the post-tryout sprints couldn't wipe the smile off Gord's face after his perfect performance. No other pitcher in camp came close to replicating his dominance. He was still walking on air as he climbed the antiquated stone steps leading to his residence. He entered Wilshire Hall with his baseball gear slung over his right shoulder and his Huron High T-shirt clinging to his exhausted, but content, body.

It was the middle of frosh week, so Gord's hall was practically a ghost town as the majority of his floor mates were ensconced in orientation activities. His room was kitty-corner to the hall entrance. He grabbed a couple of ice packs from the mini-fridge next to his desk to ice his weary arm.

He happily replayed the tryout in his mind. *Maybe they'll let me start*, Gord thought excitedly. *I could win the rookie of the year!* A knock at the hall entrance ended his daydream. Thinking that one of his floor mates had forgotten his or her key, Gord dropped his ice packs and hustled to answer the door.

A rotund, middle-aged man with snow-white hair—possessing an eerie resemblance to Santa Claus—stared back at Gord through the glass door. He was struggling with two giant tubs marked "clothes."

"Yes?" Gord inquired as his opened the door.

"I'm moving my daughter in today," Santa replied and offered an outstretched hand. "Jim Bell."

"Gord Mattis." He returned the shake. "Do you need a hand?"

"Sure. My wife and daughter are still at the car trying to organize things. You know how women are."

"I hear you," Gord replied, laughing, and picked up one of the tubs. He had assumed that all of his floor mates were moved in, but he recalled his residence adviser saying, during their first-night floor meeting, that one student had yet to arrive.

"What's your daughter's name?" Gord asked as they manoeuvred down the hall.

"Kim. We're moving her in now because she works as a counsellor at a summer camp in Oregon and just got home a week ago."

"Where are you from?"

"Orlando. We drove up and got in last night. Kim's never experienced snow before, so she wanted to go to school somewhere where there is a harsh winter. I don't get it, but it's her choice."

They stopped at Kim's door and set down the boxes on the thin, pale blue carpet.

A voice reached them from the other end of the hall. "Dad, I got the key!" Kim Bell exclaimed.

Gord turned and looked in the direction of the voice. When his eyes landed on Kim, it was like everything around him dissipated and went out of focus. Gord had never seen anyone so beautiful. Her face was unblemished perfection; like something out of a skin-care commercial. She was tall, about five foot nine, with a tanned, athletic body, and shoulder-length blonde hair, which shimmered even in the dreary residence hall lights.

"Kim, this is Gord. He's giving us a hand."

"Nice to meet you."

"Nice to meet you, too," Gord stammered. He didn't know what else to say. The girl had completely frozen his brain activity.

"Do you live on this floor as well?"

"Yeah, just, uh, just at the end of the, uh, uh, hall," Gord eventually replied. He kicked himself internally.

*Nice going, Slick.* Gord was aware of the complete nonsense coming out of his mouth, but was powerless to stop it.

"Kim, give me the key," Jim motioned to his daughter.

Kim attempted to traverse the narrow hallway, now cluttered with her tubs of clothes. Gord tried to move out of the way to clear a path for her, but she picked that exact moment to move in the same direction.

"Oh, sorry," Gord smiled sheepishly as he moved to his left.

Kim had already mirrored his move with a shift to her right, hoping to clear a path for herself. They continued with this increasingly uncomfortable dance for what seemed like an eternity, but, in reality, was only an excruciatingly long few seconds.

The awkwardness mercifully ended when Kim, laughing, grabbed Gord's bare forearms and strategically placed him to her left.

"Here, you go this way, and I'll go this way," she smiled through a dazzling set of white teeth.

Gord felt his face flush with embarrassment. He looked down at the goosebumps now covering his arms. Her touch had been electric; he had never felt anything like that before.

As Kim and Jim disappeared into the room, her infectious laugh was burned into his memory. He would give anything to be able to hear that again.

Gord didn't know what was happening to him. No high school girl had ever made him feel like Kim had in just a few seconds.

Father and daughter appeared in the threshold.

"I'll start unloading these tubs. You two go help your mom unload the rest of the van."

"No problem, Dad."

Gord was still flummoxed by their earlier exchange, but managed to steer himself after Kim as she bounced down the hallway.

Gord had no idea what to say during their walk outside to the drop-off area, but luckily, the conversation lacked any awkward pauses. Kim never stopped talking. She covered a litany of topics, while Gord dutifully smiled and nodded along. He was entranced by her vibrant outlook on life and positive, upbeat attitude. It was official: Gord Mattis was completely and utterly smitten.

He managed to mention that he played baseball and gave her the Coles Notes version of the tryout.

"You play baseball? That's awesome! I'm definitely coming to watch you play."

Gord's heart almost leapt through his chest. His smile was so wide it would have made Jack Nicholson's Joker look downright despondent in contrast.

"My boyfriend played in high school; I went to all his games. He goes to school in Kentucky."

No sooner had his heart finished its leap, it now felt like it was being crushed like a grape. It hurt to breathe. Luckily, he was able to hide his obvious disappointment. *Of course,* he thought. *How could a girl like this be available?*

The rest of the move was a blur. He vaguely remembered meeting Kim's mother and transporting what seemed like a never-ending deluge of stuff into Kim's room. Gord was in a daze. His dream girl was in a relationship. How would he handle seeing her every day on their floor?

# July 2008

## Vero Beach, Florida

Gord's eyes fluttered open.

The blinding pain of a tequila hangover made blinking a Herculean task. Lying on his side, he tried to prop himself up with his right elbow. He failed miserably, flopping back down on the thin motel mattress. At the moment, Gord's fine motor skills were non-existent.

He heard a contented sigh beside him. He slowly turned his head in the direction of the sound and noticed the unmistakable curves of a female form underneath the bedsheet.

Gord panicked. *Who the hell is that?*

He remembered nothing from the previous night except that he, in a drunken haze, stupidly thought that the best way to not get drunk on tequila was to drink *more* tequila. In hindsight, that might not have been the brightest decision.

He struggled to an upright position and peered through the darkness at Danny's bed. It was occupied by his roommate and another female body. Something bright in his peripheral vision caught his attention.

At the foot of Danny's bed, draped across the wooden chair padded with blue polyester, was Miss Duke's unforgettable yellow spaghetti-strap top. So, the case of Danny's mystery woman was solved, but Gord still had no idea who was bunked next to him.

He fumbled with the bedside alarm clock, trying to see what time it was, when a voice called out next to him.

"Good morning!" The mystery woman cheerfully chirped.

"Hey . . . you?"

"I'm surprised you're up already, after last night," she purred, reaching suggestively out to Gord underneath the covers.

It was at this moment that Gord realized he was naked. Jane Doe then mistook a regular, morning physiological occurrence as a sign of intense desire. She climbed on top of him, while Gord attempted to wriggle away.

"Since when are you so shy?" Jane Doe asked demurely.

"Uh, well, I don't want to wake them up," Gord feebly replied.

"You didn't seem to mind last night." She nodded toward the other bed. "In fact, you kept asking Jenn to join us."

Gord's clouded mind couldn't comprehend the conversation.

*Who is Jenn? And what is this woman's name? Wait. Jenn. Jenn. The other bed? Jenn must be Daisy Duke! So, this must be one of her friends from last night.*

The still nameless woman moaned as she sat down on Gord's manhood. The bed squeaked surreptitiously as she writhed above him. Gord grabbed her wrists, intent on stopping the proceedings. Jane Doe mistook it a signal to play rough. She rode him harder and harder and pinned Gord's hands behind his head.

Gord was unable to resist and rose up to meet her. They bounced up and down. Up and down. She dug her fingernails into his chest and stifled a scream. Up and down. Up and down, until they collapsed in ecstasy.

Eventually their breathing returned to normal rhythms. Lying on his chest, Jane Doe looked up at Gord and remarked, "I've never been with a professional athlete before. When are you guys back in town next?"

*Fuck. A groupie.* "Uh, well, I'll have to check the schedule. It might not be for a while," he replied, hoping she would take the hint and change the subject.

"Oh. Okay." She tried to hide her disappointment. "Can I make a call?"

"Sure."

She climbed over Gord and grabbed the phone on the nightstand. "Jenn, wake up. I'm calling for a ride."

Jenn stirred slightly, wiping the sleep out of her eyes. Danny didn't move. This was also one of his ploys. The morning after a sexual conquest, he always pretended to be passed out to avoid an awkward goodbye. This would inform potential clingy or needy women that he was interested in nothing more than a casual sexual dalliance. Usually, the girls just got fed up trying to wake him and left without a word. Childish and immature? Yes. But extremely effective.

As Gord's new friend waited for the line to make a connection, Jenn sat down on the bed next to her, trying to locate her clothes.

They were both stark naked and seemed completely at ease in their natural state. Their slim, gorgeous bodies glistened in the darkened motel room.

Gord surveyed the situation and couldn't believe his good fortune. He stifled a smile. *God, I love being a ballplayer.*

"Hey Tim, it's Jess. Can you pick Jenn and me up? We're at the Week Inn on Ocean Drive. Room 232. Thanks. See you soon."

"Who was that?" Gord inquired.

"My fiancé. He's coming to pick us up."

"Oh, okay." Gord's mind didn't register her last sentence. "Your *what*?"

"My fiancé." Jess replied matter-of-factly.

Immediately, Gord's headache cleared, but it was replaced by a deep sense of foreboding at the prospect of getting his ass kicked by a jilted lover.

"Why did you come back with us if you're engaged?" Gord tried to keep his composure.

"Why not? We're not married. I wanted to have some fun."

Gord was baffled. The logic of a groupie never ceased to amaze him. Jess's cavalier attitude toward the entire situation did little to calm his frayed nerves.

"You two have to leave. NOW." He moved quickly around the room collecting their things.

"Why? It's not a big deal."

"Yeah, well, your *fiancé* might think otherwise. If he tries to come in here and Danny somehow gets hurt, I might as well kiss my career goodbye. He's the bonus baby. If something happens to him, the front office will literally kill me."

"Don't be so dramatic. Tim's not big. He's smaller than you."

"Listen sweetheart, I'm a pitcher. I can't throw a punch with my left hand, so unless Timmy lost an arm in 'Nam, this ain't happening. You two are out of here."

Gord got the women dressed and hurried them out the door in less than five minutes. As Jess and Jenn walked down the second floor balcony, a midnight-black pickup truck peeled into the motel parking lot.

Gord pressed his nose against the window and watched the scene unfold below. From his vantage point tucked behind the musty drapes, he could see that the fiancé was not happy and kept gesturing toward the balcony. He made a start toward the staircase. Gord quickly scanned the room for some type of weapon. He spied the lamp sitting on the nightstand.

Jenn and Jess tried to block Tim from accessing the second floor. The girls were waving their arms wildly, and Tim appeared to be shouting, visibly upset. It was like watching a theatrical production of *Jerry Springer*.

Luckily, calmer heads eventually prevailed as the ladies, and a concerned motel manager, coaxed Tim back into the truck. Gord breathed a deep sigh of relief, cursing the Patron that led to such a stressful morning.

"Guys, you should have seen Gordo, peeking out the window from behind the curtains. He was scared shitless. I thought he was gonna piss his pants!"

The team laughed uproariously as Danny regaled them with his version of that morning's excitement. Johnson held court in the middle of the aisle on the bus ride back to Lakeland. Gord sat silent in his seat and shrugged his shoulders sheepishly. He knew he had looked ridiculous. His only mistake was allowing a blowhard like Danny to witness it.

"For a guy who can lift so much weight, you seemed pretty worried about that guy kicking your ass," Danny continued, baiting his roommate.

"Actually, I was more concerned about him grabbing your little buggy-whip noodle arms and tossing you out the window," Gord retorted with a cocksure smile.

"Well, this noodle arm can throw ninety-eight. Yours couldn't dent aluminum siding."

The guys howled with laughter as the insults jumped back and forth like a Wimbledon Final. Gord and Danny were at the top of their games because, as roommates, they had intricate knowledge of each other's idiosyncrasies.

"Okay, enough about this shit. I want to hear details from last night. How were the broads?" Steve Anderson inquired.

Danny, bashful as always, piped up first. "I literally ran out of things to do to that chick. She was awesome. I want to make her my

Vero Beach regular."

"Well, you spent enough money on her. Your dick owes your wallet a present," JR Coltrane quipped. "What about you, Gordo?"

"I have no idea—I don't remember a thing from last night. I didn't even know we slept together until she told me this morning."

"Really?" Chris Seaboard asked incredulously. "You should have seen yourself in the bar with her. We actually thought you two were going to fuck on the dance floor. The bouncer tossed both of you."

"You're shitting me?" Gord put his head in his hands. "I'm not drinking with you assholes again. I'm getting too old for shots."

"I'm serious," Seaboard continued. "She had her legs wrapped around you and your tongue was down her throat. He told you guys to stop or leave and get a room. So you left."

"Jesus." Gord looked at his roommate. "You're a bad influence, Danny Boy."

"Well it's about time you stopped acting like such a pussy and came out partying with us."

"Gentlemen!" Tom Conrad's voice cut through the air, and twenty-five sets of eyes focused on their manager at the front of the bus. "We've lost six of seven. That is unacceptable. We'll be back at the stadium in twenty minutes. We're going to do some running; lots of running. And we will run until I think this club's attitude has changed. Too many people here are consumed by their own stats. This is a team game, gentlemen. And we will run as a team."

The laughter immediately ceased and was replaced with groans. There's nothing baseball players hated more than running. Most of them had specifically chosen baseball as their sport of choice so they wouldn't have to run.

The five Wildcats who had gone out the previous night were now cursing that decision. Depending on Conrad's mood, there was an excellent chance the tequila would make another appearance, but this time it would be going out the way it came in.

# September 2002

## University of Michigan

KNOCK, KNOCK, KNOCK

Gord, hands folded behind his head, was in bed staring up at the dorm room ceiling. He was in a terrible mood. The knock at the door jarred him from a deep, contemplative state. He looked in the direction of the sound.

"Yeah?" he answered, annoyed.

It was ten o'clock on Sunday night, and he had just returned from a gruelling bus trip.

"It's Kim."

"Come in," he replied in a monotone. Even Kim's voice did little to raise his spirits.

Kim stepped into Gord's room, looking as beautiful as ever. She wore a form-fitting knitted sweater and a pair of charcoal-black yoga pants.

The pants were the most deceiving garment in clothing history since the advent of the padded bra. They made any ass look fantastic. A girl who had no business wearing tight jeans or dress pants would automatically have her lower half transformed into that of a fitness model. Kim already had a terrific body, so she literally turned heads when walking on campus in her yoga pants. It was as if Michelangelo himself had handcrafted her butt and thighs.

"How'd the game go?" she inquired.

"It was shit. I got crushed again." Gord sat up on the edge of the bed as Kim took a seat on his desk chair. "Coach is pulling me out of the rotation."

The University of Michigan baseball team was in the middle of their fall exhibition schedule against a selection of conference rivals. The exhibition games allowed the team to jell cohesively as a unit and gave the coaches a chance to watch the rookies cut their teeth in college ball. Plus, it gave everyone another six weeks of baseball to enjoy before the gloves were put away for the winter.

The Wolverines had just finished up a weekend series on the road against Purdue. Gord had thrown the third and final game of the series and was taken out to the woodshed. He didn't make it past the third inning, giving up five runs, six hits, and four walks.

"I'm sorry to hear that," Kim replied. "You threw so well in tryouts—what's changed?"

Since he was a kid, Gord had kept his personal problems with the game to himself. However, Kim was so easy to talk to that he was often surprised with how candid he was with her.

"I have no idea what the problem is," Gord answered honestly. "My arm feels great. These guys are just teeing off on my fastball. Plus, I can't throw my off-speed stuff for strikes and I'm always behind in the count."

The seeds of Gord's struggles were sown during his senior year of high school. His devotion to throwing hard and his love affair with strikeouts were now coming back to haunt him. Whereas high school hitters were more than willing to chase pitches off the plate, college hitters were too smart and disciplined to make the same mistake.

If Gord didn't give them a pitch to hit, they just waited for a walk. Eventually, he was forced to give in and throw "get me over" fastballs just to hit the zone. College hitters sprayed these pitches all over the park. The Purdue batters looked solely for fastballs during Gord's entire appearance, as his few attempts at a curve were looping efforts that sailed high.

Furthermore, Gord's delivery was an absolute mess. His desire to throw as hard as he could caused him to rush his mechanics. More often than not, he ended up falling off the mound toward the dugouts instead of finishing square to the plate.

"The way I'm throwing now, I'll be stuck to the bench well before the spring season begins in March. Coach isn't going to give me many more opportunities to start."

It was uncanny just how close Gord's prediction came to fruition. The winter layoff did nothing to cure his pitching woes. The more he struggled, the harder he tried to throw, and the wilder he became. It was a vicious cycle that would only be cured once he learned to be a pitcher and not a thrower.

He was relegated to the bullpen by the start of the regular season. Gord's stats for the year were unimpressive, even by freshman standards: 23IP, 15BB, 25H, 15K, 5.60 ERA. The Wolverines lost in the conference final at the end of May. Coach Picard lost so much confidence in his young rookie that Gord's last outing of the year was in mid-April versus their cross-state rivals from East Lansing. He went over six weeks without an appearance.

Back in his room, neither Kim nor Gord had any idea what was in store for Gord's first year in college baseball.

"Look," Kim began. She got up from the chair and sat down beside him, her hand resting on his knee. "I'm sure you'll turn this around; it's still early in the year."

"I hope so. After I gave up a double to my last batter, a Purdue fan stood up and yelled, 'Hey, Mattis, next outing just save yourself some time and throw it in the gap!'"

Kim couldn't help but laugh at the wit of the comment.

"Come on," she teased. "You have to admit that is pretty good."

Gord found himself smiling, despite his crummy mood. As always, Kim's laugh instantly made him feel better. His infatuation with her had not waned since the first day they had met. Although she had a boyfriend, they were each other's closest friend on the dorm floor.

Their friendship generated lots of gossip. Mutual friends thought a romance was blossoming, but, unfortunately for Gord, their relationship was completely platonic.

Sitting with her now, he could smell the citrus fragrance of her perfume. She smelled so good. The scent tickled his nostrils. Gord wanted nothing more than to tell her how he really felt but he didn't want to jeopardize their friendship.

"You're right. Thanks, Kim." Gord appreciated her efforts to cheer him up.

Kim stood up. "I'm going to bed. You're walking with me to Sociology tomorrow morning, right?"

"You bet."

"Okay, see you tomorrow. 'Night, Gord."

"'Night, Kim."

She closed the door behind her, and Gord climbed into bed with a smile on his face. His disastrous outing that afternoon was wiped from his memory. Only Kim's perfume lingered on in his mind as he drifted off to sleep.

Gord didn't pine for Kim or retreat into a shell of loneliness and heartbreak like the male lead in a second-rate 1980s chick flick. Instead, he thrust himself into the social fabric of university life. His status as a member of a varsity sports team made him an attractive commodity on the undergraduate dating landscape. Gord seemed to date a never-ending cavalcade of coeds, but he kept the relationships strictly casual. He had waited most of his adolescence to be popular with the opposite sex, so he saw no reason to commit himself to just one girl.

One story from his freshman year solidified Gord's reputation as a proficient dater among his baseball brethren and garnered him somewhat legendary status in his residence hall.

In late October, Brent McPhee and his housemates threw a kegger to celebrate the end of mid-term exams. It was a party for primarily senior students. Returning to the scene of his infamous rookie night, Gord was one of a few underclassmen in attendance. He was in the kitchen, talking shop with Matt Carbone and John Sukrage, when he heard a female voice call out his name from across the room.

"Gord? What are you doing here?" A tall, slim brunette led three girls back toward the guys.

"Hey, Alex, what's up?" Gord was surprised to see her. "I play ball with one of the guys who lives here."

Alexandra Opal was the resident adviser on Gord's floor. It was rare that they saw each other outside of the confines of their hall. Being at the same party was just plain weird. They were both a tad wary of hanging out in the same social circle.

Alexandra, being in a position of authority, didn't want one of her charges to see her engage in behaviour that she had decried in one of many RA lectures. Likewise, Gord didn't want to do anything stupid in the vicinity of his resident adviser.

"Cool," Alexandra replied. "These are my friends Rachel, Elle, and Darci. Gord's one of the guys on my floor."

Gord introduced Carbone and Sukrage to Alexandra and her

friends. The group shared some similar classes and mutual friends, so the conversation was smooth and free-flowing. Eventually, they all headed to the living room, where games of Flip Cup were being held.

"I don't think this is such a good idea," Alexandra remarked as the guys organized the cups of beer. "I shouldn't be drinking with you, Gord. You're one of my kids."

"Come on, Alex, it's not a big deal."

"No, I'm going to go do a lap." She gave a look to her friends. "You guys stay and play."

The three Wolverines challenged the three girls to a battle of the sexes Flip Cup challenge. They decided on a best of seven series. The guys' aim was twofold: one, to show their Flip Cup dominance; two, to get the girls drunk enough so they'd be willing to make questionable decisions later on.

Unfortunately, they severely underestimated the prowess of girls with three plus years of college life under their belts. The ladies were Flip Cup dynamos. What they lacked in chugging ability, they made up for with masterful flipping. Also, the guys had Gord on their team who, as a freshman, lacked necessary skills—he got drunk way too fast and quickly became useless as a flipper.

Gord was matched against Rachel in the anchor position. She was extremely friendly and talkative. Even through his alcoholic haze, Gord could tell that Rachel had been eyeing him pretty voraciously between games.

However, Gord was unsure how to proceed. This was uncharted territory for him at this point in his college career. He had primarily dated freshman girls. A senior taking an interest in him was not something he expected.

The Wolverines pulled out a hard-fought victory in the seventh game, when Gord's cup rested upside down on the table a fraction of a second before Rachel's. After a wild celebration of fist bumps and man hugs, the guys shook the hands of their opponents.

Rachel pulled Gord away from the rest of the group and into one of the adjoining rooms. She gazed hungrily into his eyes as they sat together on a loveseat. Gord struggled to think of something to say to ease his nervousness.

"So, uh, how do you know Alexandra?"

"We've known each other since first year. I'm an RA in Wilshire, too. Up on five."

"Cool. Where are you from?"

Rachel tousled Gord's hair. "You're really cute, you know that?"

Gord tried to think of something witty to retort, but his mind wasn't working properly. "You're not doing too bad yourself."

She laughed. "You're quite the sweet talker." Rachel moved toward Gord and rested her hand on his upper thigh.

"I, uh, do what I can . . ."

Kicking himself internally, Gord realized that the less he said, the better. It was obvious Rachel liked being the aggressor, so he decided to keep his mouth shut and let her dictate the pace.

"Come here," she purred.

Rachel clasped her hands around Gord's neck and kissed him on the lips. *Jackpot*, Gord thought. After a few minutes, she stopped and pulled away from him. He looked at her quizzically.

"Want to get out of here?" She winked.

Gord was ecstatic but tried to play it cool. "Sure, let's go."

Rachel took him by the hand, and they left the kegger without a word to their friends. Back in his dorm room, Gord was given a crash course in sex with a dominant woman. He was used to demure, teenaged girls. Rachel was a twenty-two-year-old woman who knew exactly what she wanted.

Gord awoke to see Rachel getting dressed quietly at the foot of his bed.

"What time is it?" he asked sleepily.

"It's ten. I'm going to take off. This was fun." She crawled toward him and kissed him deeply, her tongue exploring Gord's mouth.

"I'll walk you out." He threw on a pair of boxer shorts and escorted Rachel toward the door.

As they stood at the threshold of his room, a group of Gord's floor mates, led by Alexandra, were returning from breakfast at the university cafeteria.

Alexandra stopped dead in her tracks and stared incredulously at the two of them. Gord and Rachel stared back, sheepish grins on their faces. An awkward silence hung in the air for what seemed like an eternity.

"What are you doing here, Rachel?" Alexandra demanded.

"Gord, apparently," one of the students quipped.

Alexandra shot the smartass a hard look.

"It's not a big deal, Alex," Rachel nonchalantly replied. "Don't worry about it."

"It *is* a big deal, Rachel. He's a student on my floor."

Alexandra whirled her gaze to a visibly uncomfortable Gord. He had his arms folded across his bare chest and tried his best to avert his eyes from Alexandra's probing stare. The students behind Alexandra looked excitedly at one another, in disbelief at the juicy gossip unfolding in front of them.

"I'll talk to both of you later," Alexandra continued through gritted teeth. She brushed past them and made a beeline for her room at the end of the hall.

"I should go, too." Rachel stepped through the group of freshmen like Moses parting the Red Sea.

After she was out of earshot, two of the guys in the group excitedly approached Gord.

"Dude, isn't she an RA in this building?" the first one asked.

Gord nodded.

"Nice job, Gordo!" said the other, slapping him a high-five.

Gord's extracurricular activity with the RA spread like wildfire throughout the ball team as Carbone and Sukrage grilled him for details at the next team outing. Gord's reputation as a player was cemented.

Kim, cognizant of his exploits, asked Gord why he engaged in such promiscuous behaviour. Wanting to mask his true feelings toward her, he compared college dating life to eating at a buffet. "You don't go to the Golden Corral and eat only one dish. I want to try everything on the menu."

However, the real reason why Gord's first year "relationships" all fizzled out so quickly was that he found himself comparing every girl to Kim. As soon as Gord realized that the girl fell short of Kim in terms of intelligence, personality, sense of humour, et cetera, he automatically dumped her and looked for someone else. He tried to distance himself from his true feelings toward Kim by dating different girls, but he soon came to a disturbing conclusion. What if no woman would ever make him feel the way he did when he first laid eyes on Kim?

# July 2008

## Orlando, Florida

After the piss-poor performance in Vero Beach, Tom Conrad, as promised, put the team through a series of diabolical conditioning drills when the Wildcats returned to Lakeland. After forty-five long minutes of shuttle runs and wind sprints, Conrad mercifully ended the punishment and left the majority of his players lying in the outfield grass gasping for air. The late July sun, coupled with the oppressive Florida humidity, made it feel like they were running on the surface of the sun.

But the drills had the desired effect on the team as the Wildcats embarked on a five-game home-winning streak the next day. Lakeland fired on all cylinders during the homestand: the offence hit over .300 with runners in scoring position, the pitching staff had an ERA under 3.00, and the defence had their longest errorless streak of the season.

Gord appeared in two games during the winning streak. Technically, he cobbled together a stat line considered a "quality start" by the baseball intelligentsia: 6 innings pitched and 3 earned runs.

A quality start was recognized as giving up three runs or less in six or more innings pitched. Truthfully, it was a pointless statistic created by the math nerds who ran the baseball operations of most clubs.

Gord, like most pitchers, didn't take solace in the fact he produced a quality start. Why? Because three earned runs in six innings computed to a 4.50 ERA. A pitcher should never be satisfied with an ERA above four. In the minor leagues, a 4.50 earned run average got you pink-slipped out of the game.

*You show me a pitcher happy with meeting the minimum requirement for a quality start, and I'll show you a loser*, Gord thought.

The Wildcats were en route to the Global Sports Complex for the first game in a series against the Orlando Buccaneers. Gord, listening to his iPod, read the stat sheets on the opposing lineup. Tom

Conrad had told him to be ready to pitch a couple of innings.

Danny Johnson suddenly appeared at Gord's side and playfully whacked him on the shoulder.

"What's up, Danny?" Gord removed his earbuds.

"You throwing tonight?"

"Yeah, Tom has me scheduled to throw a few. Why?"

"Put those babies down," Johnson quipped, motioning to the stat sheets. "I'm starting tonight, and my arm feels fucking unreal. I'm going at least eight."

"Sure thing, Ace."

"Mark me down for at least twelve punchouts, too. Maybe you can make a bunch of little K signs while watching my dominance from the bullpen."

"Do you want me to call ahead to the Buccaneers and tell them to not bother showing up?"

"Funny guy. I'll let you get back to your Hannah Montana CD."

Gord laughed heartily. "Okay, buddy, go sit down. You don't want to tire yourself out before all of those strikeouts."

Lakeland was up 5–0 in the top of the eighth inning. To say Danny Johnson was cruising did not do his performance justice. He was destroying the Buccaneers. Not only was his fastball sitting consistently at ninety-five with late life, his curveball was an absolute hammer.

After each strikeout, Danny would spin off the mound and give a little point to Gord, sitting in the Wildcats' bullpen down the left field line. Gord could do nothing but shake his head in amazement at his precocious roommate.

The seventh inning ended with Danny's thirteenth punchout of the game. Gord waved a white towel in recognition of Danny's uncanny prediction and to signify his submission. Danny pointed at Gord one last time as he skipped off the field to soak up the adoration from his impressed teammates and coaching staff.

Amazingly, Danny had thrown only eighty-four pitches through seven innings, despite all of the strikeouts. He was startlingly efficient. Danny had faced only one three-ball count all night and had relinquished only two infield singles.

Steve Anderson shouted down to Gord from the other end of the bullpen bench, "You better get comfy, Gordo. There's no way any of us are getting near that mound. This is Danny's night."

"Yeah, no shit. I'm riding the pine pony for the rest of the game."

"What's the team record for strikeouts in a game?" Anderson asked no one in particular.

"Fifteen," Jeff Merkle piped up.

"He's getting that for sure," Anderson replied.

A call came in over the bullpen phone. Tim Reid snatched it up before it had a chance to ring twice.

"Mattis!" the Badger growled. "Johnson's finishing this game. Warm up and throw a bullpen down here to stay sharp."

Gord had already thrown long toss and stretched before the game, so his body was basically warm. However, his arm and shoulder were slightly stiff from sitting on the bench for seven innings.

The few hundred fans scattered around the ballpark were in the middle of an off-key rendition of "Take Me Out to the Ball Game" for the seventh inning stretch. Gord stood up and joined them.

He made slow arm circles forward, loosening his joints. The circles got progressively bigger and faster, while he tested the limits of his range of motion. Next, he grabbed his glove and inserted two baseballs into the webbing. With the glove in a pincer grip in his throwing hand, Gord bent over at the waist and swung his arm forward and backward between his legs.

Then, he made clockwise circles from the same position. He stood upright and dangled his pitching arm at his side. He raised his left arm until it was perpendicular to the ground and returned it to the starting position for a total of twelve repetitions. Swinging his arm straight out in front of his body, he began making figure eights with his weighted glove, stretching the small muscles of his forearm and increasing the motility of his elbow ligaments.

At this point, the rest of the pitching staff stared at Gord in bemused wonderment. They always got a kick out of Gord's intricate stretching ritual and needled him about his obsessive behaviour. Sometimes they deliberately miscounted out loud, hoping to mess with his rhythm.

Gord knew he looked goofy, but he'd done the stretches since he was in high school. If he skipped them, he felt uncomfortable on the mound. The last thing a pitcher needed was concern over whether or not his arm was warmed up enough.

The final stretch of Gord's routine once again had him bent over at the waist. He aggressively swung his left arm from in front of his body to directly overhead. He repeated the process ten times in rapid succession. It made him look like a wind turbine.

Sufficiently warmed up, he headed to the bullpen mound. At the same time, Danny jumped out of the dugout and raced to the middle of the diamond for the bottom of the eighth. Gord gave a quick nod to backup catcher Aaron Carmack, indicating that he was ready to begin throwing.

With one eye on the field watching Johnson's assault on Lakeland's strikeout record, Gord lightly tossed with Carmack, who was crouched behind the plate. Gord's first ten throws were slow, arcing fastballs. Their purpose was to establish a solid mechanical base before he increased velocity. Once Gord was confident that he could replicate his delivery, he motioned to Carmack that he was going to start throwing harder. Coincidentally, Danny had just finished his own warm-up pitches and was about to deliver the first pitch of the inning.

Carmack set up on the corner of the plate, adjacent to the left-handed batter's box. Gord peppered fastballs at 80 percent velocity into this vicinity over and over again. Carmack rarely moved his mitt. They repeated the same process on the other side of the plate.

Danny struck out the first batter of the eighth on four pitches. Fourteen strikeouts. The second hitter, the Buccaneers' leadoff man, flared an opposite field single to short right field. This marked the first time all game Orlando's offence was able to "touch green."

The third batter of the inning worked the count to 2 and 2. Danny momentarily forgot about the runner on first base and threw the fifth pitch of the at-bat from a full windup. The runner took second base uncontested, while the pitch was in the dirt for ball three.

With a commanding lead, Lakeland's infield good-naturedly bashed Johnson for his brain fart.

"Hey, stay hot, kid!"

"We throw from the stretch in this league, Bonus Baby!"

"That steal's on you, Johnson!"

"That's a fine!" Steve Anderson yelled from the bullpen. Gord laughed and nodded in agreement.

The incident would undoubtedly be addressed at the next hearing of Lakeland's Kangaroo Court.

Dave Rockwood called time and went to the mound to chat with a sheepish-looking Danny. Rockwood wanted to calm his pitcher down and tell Danny to forget about the mental error. He also needed to remind Danny of the signs with a runner on second. This was the first time a runner had reached second base all game, so Rockwood wanted to make sure they were on the same page.

When play resumed, the Wildcats' battery decided to go with a 3–2 off-speed pitch. Danny snapped off a backdoor curve that fooled the hitter, but bent around the plate. Ball four.

Runners were now on first and second. Danny kicked the dirt in front of the mound in disgust, angry at himself for relinquishing his first walk of the night. He took a deep breath. There was no way he was going to lose his shutout on a mental mistake and a walk.

Quickly getting ahead of the next hitter 0–2, Danny was poised to tie the team record. He reared back and let fly with a high, outside fastball. The batter was looking heat, but with two strikes could only muster a short, protective swing.

He sent a humpback liner toward second base. The runners moved on contact, as the Buccaneers wanted nothing more than to break their goose egg. Lakeland's shortstop, Chris Mills, drifted over, snared the ball, and touched second base. Double play. Inning over.

As the Wildcats hustled in for the top of the ninth, Gord continued his work in the bullpen. He worked on two types of curveballs: backdoor hammers that right-handed hitters gave up on and big breakers that bisected the middle of the plate, leaving left-handed hitters with jelly in their legs. Carmack kept his glove eight inches off the ground. He wanted Gord's breaking balls to finish low in the zone, out of harm's way in a real game.

The Wildcats went down suspiciously fast in their half of the ninth. Everyone wanted to get the game over with and see what Danny had in store for his final inning. Though the home team faced a five-run deficit, the crowd was still very much into the game. They understood what a rare opportunity it was to witness such an incredible pitching performance.

On the mound, Danny wore his heart on his sleeve, and tonight was no different. He paced around the hill, waiting for his teammates to finish slinging the ball around the horn. He hopped up and down like a prizefighter, waiting for the batter to take his position in the box.

At this juncture in the game, Danny was too charged up and jittery to be able to finesse off-speed pitches over the plate. No, he was going to finish this game off with his best pitch: a darting fastball that occasionally threatened triple digits.

Back in the bullpen, Gord began the final phase of his throwing regimen: a simulated inning where the pitches, balls, and strikes were called by Aaron Carmack. Since there were no batters, Gord instituted a unique set of rules for this exercise. There were no walks. In the event of a fourth ball, it was assumed that the batter fouled the pitch off, no matter where the ball was located.

The requirements for what constituted a strike were extremely stringent. The zone stretched from mid-shin to upper thigh; anything above crotch level was deemed too high and called a ball. This forced Gord to work in the bottom half of the strike zone. He had to live down there to be successful. This exercise drilled that maxim into his head and forced his release point to adjust accordingly.

Danny faced the bottom third of the Buccaneers' order in the home half of the ninth. Orlando's seventh hitter was a wispy, freakishly strong kid from the Dominican Republic. He could hit the ball a mile, but his swing was way too long and overly aggressive to make consistent contact. He corkscrewed himself into the dirt after every swing.

Three fastballs up in the zone later, each one higher than the last, and Mighty Casey had struck out for the third time in the game. Fifteen punchouts for Danny, which tied Lakeland's team record.

Gord worked through his simulated inning with surgical precision. Each pitch he threw lived on the outer edges of the plate. Carmack never raised his glove higher than sixteen inches off the dirt.

Every player on the Wildcats' roster was on the top step of the dugout shouting encouragement at their ace. The crowd cheered every strike call by the umpire. They no longer had an allegiance to the Buccaneers. They were now just fans of the game.

Dave Rockwood wasn't even giving signs at this point. He just held his mitt out as a target and waited for Danny to burn in another fastball. The count ran to 1–2 on the second hitter of the inning. Danny reared back and painted the outside corner with a two-seam fastball. The pitch had started outside and the hitter gave up on it. He was flummoxed to see the ball run right back over the black.

The radar gun behind home plate registered ninety-six miles per hour. Danny was throwing just as hard in his last inning as he was in his first. The bat never left the hitter's shoulder. The home plate umpire thrust his right arm into the air. Sixteen.

Gord focused his attention on Carmack's glove and finished off his session with two wonderful changeups that dipped and dived down low, a fraction of an inch off the plate.

Watching Danny pump fastballs and be successful, while he had to bite and nibble, was an ironic moment not lost on Gord. He realized that, while they were on the same pitching staff, he and Danny were solar systems apart in terms of their baseball ability and eventual career arc. It was unlikely Danny would still be in A ball by Labour Day. A promotion to Double A seemed imminent.

On the other hand, Gord was barely treading water in Lakeland. Pitchers with his stuff were a dime a dozen. While he had begun to show signs of improvement from earlier in the year, how much of it was attributed to his being so much older and more experienced than the young, free-swinging lineups he faced on a nightly basis? Was he getting hitters out with talent, or was it just guile and a high baseball IQ acquired through more years of seasoning?

Gord joined the rest of the bullpen on the bench to watch Danny put the finishing touches on his masterpiece. Wanting to end with a flourish, Danny deserted his mechanics and threw the first two pitches way out of the strike zone. 2–0.

"Come on, Danny, stay on top of the ball. Finish square to the plate," Gord chided softly. He turned to face Aaron Carmack. "Rockwood should go talk to him."

Sure enough, Lakeland's catcher called time and jogged out to the mound for a quick conference with his hurler. Danny nodded in agreement with his catcher's words. Rockwood patted Danny lightly on the back and returned behind the plate.

The chat worked. Danny quickly evened the count at 2–2. Focusing all of his energy into one last pitch, he took a deep breath, came set, and fired. The batter had no chance. The ninety-eight-mile-an-hour fastball was practically in Rockwood's glove before the hitter had a chance to start his swing.

Seventeen strikeouts! A new team record! Danny pumped his fist in victory. He met his catcher halfway between the mound and the plate, and thanked Rockwood for calling such a terrific game. Lakeland's bench emptied as the team rushed out to congratulate their ace. The guys in the bullpen hopped off the bench and joined the fray on the field. Jogging to meet the rest of the team, Gord smiled, thoroughly impressed with the pitching prowess of his roommate.

He knew that he would never be able to match Danny's electric stuff. But, as he demonstrated during his bullpen session, Gord had the ability to put the ball wherever he wanted when he was "on." In fact, it was this ability to throw strikes that led to his employment in minor league baseball in the first place. Without his transition from a thrower to a true pitcher, Gord's baseball dream would have ended long before the end of his university career.

# February 2004

## Lubbock, Texas
## Dan Law Field

"Dude, my arm is killing me." Gord feverishly tried to shake off the dull ache that reverberated from his left shoulder down to his elbow.

"What do you want to do?" freshman catcher Jeremy McLeod asked. "Should we tell Coach?"

They were standing in the enclosed bullpen on the home field of Texas Tech University. The Wolverines had begun their spring season in the Texas Tech tournament to open the 2004 campaign. With two starters lost to graduation, Wolverine manager Perry Picard was giving his left-handed sophomore one final shot at the rotation. Gord hoped to rebound after a dismal rookie season.

"No, don't say anything. This might be my last chance to be a starter. I can't tell him how I hurt my arm."

The night before, a group of Wolverines had gone to an adult arcade complex in downtown Lubbock. It had a pitching video simulation game that documented the speed of pitches. Gord, flush with liquid courage and his stubborn obsession with velocity, tried to set the arcade record for fastest pitch. With no warm-up, he began firing balls at the target with reckless abandon. His top speed was eighty-five. That set the machine record, although none of his teammates were dumb enough to follow suit.

The next morning, Gord's left arm throbbed. He downed a few Tylenols, which initially seemed to help, but was forced to halt his bullpen session halfway through to rest his weary arm.

"Can you even pitch?" McLeod was skeptical. "You're not throwing very hard at all. If you don't keep the ball down, these guys will tee off on you. Then you really won't be a starter."

Gord shook his head. "I don't care. If I say I'm hurting and someone else starts this game and throws a gem, I'm toast. I have to do this."

McLeod contemplated his pitcher. A rookie from Des Moines, Iowa, he was only getting the start behind the plate because it was the last game of the exhibition tournament and Coach Picard wanted to rest Matt Carbone, the first-string catcher.

Though he was just a freshman, McLeod was supremely talented defensively. Plus, he was a throwback to a different era. McLeod was an old-school baseball player. He wasn't flashy or consumed with personal success—he just wanted to help his team win ball games any way he could. It was cliché, but McLeod "played the game the right way." Gord could tell, from just a few short bullpen sessions, that the rookie called a terrific game.

A great catcher could save a pitcher a few outs every game just from the way he conducted himself behind the dish. If a pitcher had supreme confidence in his battery mate, then he could focus all of his concentration on throwing strikes and not let any extraneous thoughts enter his mind.

"Okay, let's do it." McLeod pulled down his face mask. "Just hit my glove. I'll take care of the rest."

Gord nodded appreciatively and gritted his way through the rest of his warm-up.

Once the game began, Gord was a completely different pitcher from his rookie season. His velocity dropped significantly due to the pain in his arm, but all he cared about was throwing strikes and being economical in his pitch count. The fewer pitches he threw, the less his arm hurt.

No longer looking for strikeouts, Gord was now pitching to contact. He didn't worry about trying to throw the ball through McLeod. Instead, he just played catch with him and focused on hitting the mitt. Gord didn't rush his mechanics like he usually did when he tried to throw hard. Now, he just ensured that his delivery was sound and his timing was impeccable.

The smooth delivery, combined with the drop in velocity, was the main reason why Gord was able to tolerate the pain in his arm. If he maintained a consistent release point, then each pitch didn't feel like someone had jammed a knife into the back of his shoulder and the inside of his elbow.

Michigan's opponent was the Jacksonville State Gamecocks. The game was scoreless after three innings and maintained a breakneck pace of play—only forty minutes had elapsed since the first pitch. The Wolverines' battery was primarily responsible for the quick pace, as Gord had yet to shake off a sign set down by Jeremy McLeod. They were completely in sync, and Gord was absolutely shredding through the Gamecocks' lineup.

He was perfect through three innings, with a seven-to-two ground ball to fly ball ratio. Gord delivered a first pitch strike to eight of nine batters and did not have one three-ball count.

Bumping fists with his teammates in the dugout during the top of the fourth, Gord was amazed at his performance thus far. McLeod settled down beside him and lowered his voice.

"How's the arm?"

"It hurts, but I'm managing."

"You're pitching great; just keep throwing strikes."

"It's incredible. I've never had command like this. It feels like I can throw it wherever I want."

"Because you're just trying to throw strikes." McLeod slowed his words to emphasize his point. "You're pitching instead of throwing."

"Yeah. Who gives a shit about strikeouts? This is fun. I'm just going to let the defence do all the work."

The Wolverines made the third out of their half inning. McLeod grabbed his mask and tapped Gord on the thigh. "Okay, let's go."

Gord mowed down the Jacksonville hitters in the bottom of the fourth and continued his dominance in the fifth. His transformation to a true pitcher was complete. Picard pulled him after five innings. Gord had thrown seventy pitches, which was the predetermined pitch count imposed on all pitchers during the month of February.

Gord went from a possible pitching staff footnote to weaving five perfect innings against one of the top twenty-five offences in the country.

The outing not only proved to the Wolverines' coaching staff that Gord could handle a spot in the rotation, but it cemented McLeod's position as Gord's personal catcher. They were on the same page right from the first pitch. There was a comfort level between the two of them that sometimes took an entire season to develop.

When the Wolverines returned home from the southern leg of spring training, Gord was pencilled in as the number three starter. His college baseball career was beginning to show some promise, and that positive energy transferred over to his social and educational life as well.

Up to that point, the second year of Gord's university experience had been excellent. He lived off campus with three other guys from the baseball team in housing designated solely for varsity athletes and maintained by the university.

Gord decided to declare his major in physical education. He had seen first-hand how the benefits of strength and physical conditioning had been a boon to his baseball career. Therefore, he wanted to stay on the cutting edge of new developments in exercise science, so he'd have an advantage over guys with greater talent.

University athletes received certain advantages when it came to academic expectations and course loads. Gord and his teammates had no concept of due dates. They could hand in assignments late and still have the opportunity to receive full credit. Free tutors were made available at all times, and a paper completed by an athlete was always marked with a more lenient hand than one written by a member of the general student population.

Thus, for the entire first semester, Gord and his housemates focused primarily on the following: off-season training, drinking and partying, and getting laid. Still, these extracurricular activities had no effect on Gord's grades. His knack for kinesiology enabled him to pull a 3.5 grade-point average at the end of first term.

Gord's friendship with Kim was still strong, and his infatuation with her had not waned at all in the year they had known each other. Their relationship had taken a slight detour from strictly platonic to a weird, grey area: an area where it was apparent that one of the parties involved was looking for something more than being "just friends." Gord, not as nervous and anxious around Kim as he'd been as a freshman, made it quite obvious that he was physically attracted to her. He flirted with Kim suggestively, but still kept a respectful distance because he valued their friendship so highly.

Kim easily ascertained Gord's interest level, but she, considering his dismal track record with relationships, didn't read much into his flirtations. Kim misguidedly perceived Gord's interest as just wanting another notch on his bedpost. Still dating her boyfriend, Kim didn't look at Gord and see relationship material. To her, they were friends and that was all.

One night at the end of March, Gord walked Kim home after a party at Tap Tavern with some of their floor mates from first year. Gord was riding high from his scoreless innings streak to start the season. Since that first outing in Lubbock, when Gord was forced to concentrate on throwing strikes and pitching to contact, he had not given up a run. Throughout the Wolverines' entire spring training trip, he had spun twenty-five consecutive scoreless innings, five off the team record.

Looking up at the night sky, illuminated by the full moon, Gord figured this was his chance to find out where he stood with Kim. He glanced over at her as they walked. Kim's face shone in the moonlight. She was so beautiful. Needing some time to organize his thoughts, Gord stopped in front of Joe's Pita.

"Do you want to grab a pita? My treat."

"Sure!" Kim exclaimed. "Sounds good."

The place was packed. Joe's Pita was full of partiers looking to sop up the excess alcohol flooding their systems with some post-bar food. Amid the boisterous chatter, Gord and Kim ordered their pitas.

"Should we eat and walk?" Kim asked, as she took her pita from the stressed employee manning the grill.

"Let's grab a table. I think I saw an open one at the back."

They traversed the narrow passageway and moved through the throng of like-minded students. Their table was set back from the crowd and provided a respite from the noise. As they ate, Gord suddenly clammed up. He was unsure of what to say or how to begin. He wanted to find out if there could ever be a romantic future between them, but he couldn't find the words.

Luckily, Kim talked enough for both of them. She was a chatterbox when completely sober. After a few drinks, Kim's speech resembled the rat-tat-tat of a machine gun. She talked continually, about anything and everything.

Gord found himself goofily grinning at Kim. This was the feeling he had searched for with his assembly line of one-night stands and meaningless hookups.

Kim noticed the absent-minded grin on his face. "Why are you smiling at me like that?"

"What? Oh well, I—uh . . ."

"Just tell me." She smiled back. "You can tell me anything."

"Well," Gord began, placing his pita down on the wooden tabletop, "I was just wondering if, uh, there was, uh, a chance that you and I would, you know, ever get together."

Kim was silent for the first time since they sat down. She considered Gord to be one of her closest friends at school. In fact, he was probably the best male friend she had in the entire state of Michigan.

After what seemed like an eternity, Kim finally responded. "I'm not sleeping with you, Gord." She broke out into a broad smile. "Call one of your little pop tart baseball groupies for that. Nice try, though; you had me going for a second there."

"What?" Gord was perturbed. "No, I'm serious."

"Really?"

"Yes."

"You're not just saying this because you're drunk and you didn't pick up tonight and I just happen to be here with you now?"

"No, I mean it." Gord was uncharacteristically serious. "Could something ever happen between us?"

Kim didn't know how to answer. Periodically, she had wondered the same thing. Why couldn't she tell Gord that? They got along so well and they laughed at the same silly jokes. Could they make that transition from friends to something more? Kim tried to skirt the issue.

"Gord, I'm still with James. We're happy together."

"I know you are. It's just—it felt like something I needed to ask."

"You're one of my best friends here. I wouldn't want to jeopardize that, even if I was single."

"Okay," Gord mumbled, crushed. "I'm sorry. I shouldn't have brought it up."

Gord realized the conversation had taken a heavy turn. He needed to keep things light so that Kim couldn't tell how much her rejection hurt him. He decided to deflect the inner turmoil churning around in his gut and lighten the mood with an infusion of humour. He flashed Kim a cocksure grin. "So, I guess things are going to be really awkward between us?"

She welcomed the deflection. "Oh, absolutely. I'm definitely going to be weird around you now."

"Sweet. Actually, maybe we should just sleep together. We have nothing to lose."

"You're an idiot." Kim laughed that infectious chuckle Gord found so irresistible. "Walk me home, Romeo."

They both stood up. Gord offered his arm to Kim in an overly dramatic, cheesy gesture. Still laughing, she pushed him away and started out the door.

"You're such a dork!"

He followed her outside. He shrugged his shoulders. *Well, you gave it a shot. A valiant effort, Gordo*, he told himself.

# June 2004

## Corvallis, Oregon
## Goss Stadium

*He's powerless to stop it. The crowd's taunts become more derisive and vitriolic. The boos thunder down onto the field and rattle Gord's eardrums.*

*The walks and runs pile up like stacks of cordwood. Gord looks in desperation to the bullpen, longing for relief and an end to the nightmare, but no one is there. He is completely and utterly alone . . .*

Gord's cleats crunched over the crushed rock encircling Goss Stadium, home of the Oregon State Beavers. He jogged along the warning track, the stifling humidity soaking his warm-up shirt with rivers of sweat. His teammates finished batting practice while he ran.

Ordinarily, he would take part and shag flies, but not today. Today, Gord was a beacon of focus. Nothing entered his mind but the task at hand: the Game 1 start in the regional championships.

Most teams would have been wary of starting a true sophomore in such a pressure-packed situation, but Coach Picard had no such reservations. Gord had followed his stellar exhibition season with a regular season campaign unmatched by any other hurler on Michigan's pitching staff.

And he did it by keeping things simple. Gord followed the lesson he had learned in February at Texas Tech: throw strikes, don't worry about throwing hard all the time, and pitch to contact. By slowing down his delivery and acquiring a consistent release point, he was finally able to get control of his off-speed pitches. He had the confidence to throw his changeup and curveball in any count. His fastball held in the mid-eighties, but he was able to flirt with eighty-eight or eighty-nine, if he really reached back for something extra.

Gord owed the majority of his success to his battery mate, Jeremy McLeod. McLeod had the uncanny ability to calm Gord down in pressure situations. He coached Gord through outings when he didn't have his best stuff. With runners on, Gord tended to revert back to his old ways. He tried to overpower hitters to get out of jams. McLeod was able to convince him to slow things down when pressed. Trust your stuff, take deep breaths, and concentrate on making good pitches, McLeod told him. Make batters hit your pitch. Don't worry about speed, worry about strikes.

McLeod caught Gord every time he pitched, regardless of the circumstance. The decision was somewhat controversial, as Matt Carbone was one of the team's leading hitters and McLeod had a weak bat, but Picard didn't want to mess with the magic of the Mattis/McLeod combination.

They had an almost telepathic relationship. Teammates marvelled at how the duo rarely required mound visits to discuss strategy, and no one could recall the last time Gord shook off a signal put down by McLeod.

Gord's stats for the year were incredibly impressive: 65 strikeouts in 85 innings, with only 12 walks and a 2.29 ERA. He had also won eight games and lost only three.

Without question, Gord deserved the Game 1 start, but Oregon State was nationally ranked in the top ten. Plus, Goss Stadium was a tough venue for any visiting pitcher, let alone a twenty-year-old sophomore. There were thousands of Oregon State students ready to make Gord's life a living hell once he took the mound.

It was the biggest start of Gord's young life.

"Ready?" McLeod asked, as they trotted into the bullpen to warm up.

"You bet. You and me. Let's get it done."

With that, McLeod squatted down behind the plate, and Gord toed the bullpen rubber. He fired in a fastball right at his catcher's mitt. It perfectly bisected McLeod's body.

"Atta baby," McLeod cried as he tossed the ball back. "Right there, all day!"

The Wolverines congregated around Perry Picard in Michigan's dugout.

"Gentlemen. You know what you have to do. There's not much I have to say. Let's get on the sticks early and take the crowd out of the game. We have Gordie on the bump; strong defence behind him. Okay, hands in." Picard stuck his hand in the middle of the circle, and his charges obliged him.

Brent McPhee, last year's captain and new graduate assistant on Michigan's coaching staff, led the team in their pregame cheer.

"Okay, boys. This is our first trip to the regionals in a decade. Let's do it. 'Wolverines' on three. One, two, three . . . WOLVERINES!" Their cheer, loud and hearty, cut through the burgeoning masses in cavernous Goss Stadium. Michigan was the personification of focused determination.

The Wolverines were up first. Gord watched his team take their first hacks from the far end of the dugout. He paced around anxiously. The adrenaline coursing through his veins made it impossible for him to sit still.

McPhee, the team comedian and renowned pop culture buff, approached. Wanting to keep his starter loose, McPhee took Gord by the shoulders and looked him right in the eye.

"Gord, you look a little tense." McPhee paused for dramatic effect. "Remember, you . . . are my number one . . . guy!"

Gord looked at his former teammate quizzically. "What?"

"It's from *Batman*. The first one. Jack Nicholson as the Joker."

"Uh, okay."

"Never mind." McPhee was used to his obscure references going over the players' heads. "Just go kick some ass."

Gord smiled at his assistant coach. "Why didn't you just say that in the first place?"

The Wolverines went down in order in the top of the first. Gord grabbed his glove and marched the length of the dugout. He bumped fists with McLeod just outside the foul line and jogged to the mound.

McLeod whipped Gord's last warm-up pitch down to second baseman Paul Pena, who started the ball around the horn. The white pearl nestled in third baseman TJ Jackson's glove. Jackson stood a few feet from his pitcher on the green synthetic turf at the back of the mound.

"Shut 'em down, Gordie!" Jackson shouted, flipping him the ball.

Gord massaged it between his bare hands and took his position on top of the world. The red clay of the mound stained his sparkling blue and white spikes. The crowd swelled in anticipation of Oregon's first opportunity at bat.

Gord took a deep, relaxing breath. The year before, the crowd and magnitude of the situation would have caused him to overthrow. He would have tried to impress everyone with his velocity. Not anymore. Now, he was just looking to throw strikes. Now, he was a pitcher.

Sixty feet, six inches away, McLeod flashed a sign. Cognizant of the "old Gord," McLeod called for a first pitch changeup to force Gord to slow down and not rush his delivery. With the crowd buzzing in his ears and the Beavers on the top step of their dugout hollering at him, Gord stepped back with his right foot to start his windup.

The first hitter was right-handed, so McLeod set up on the outside corner and pushed his glove downward, indicating he wanted the pitch to finish low and away. Gord's fingers slid over the ball and he snapped his wrist upon releasing the pitch. The ball started over the middle of the plate, but the spin from his hand forced it toward McLeod's mitt. Gravity did the rest.

The batter, wanting to jump on Gord and the Wolverines early, was looking fastball and started his swing too early. His bat flailed through the zone and the ball settled neatly in McLeod's glove. Strike one.

The next pitch was an inside fastball, which the batter chopped toward Paul Pena. Pena scooped it up cleanly and fired the ball to first for the out. The second and third hitters in Oregon State's lineup followed with a fly ball to left and a soft liner to Jackson at the hot corner. Three up, three down.

The game was scoreless after seven innings. The tension in the stadium increased considerably. It was apparent that one run would more than likely be enough to win the game.

Both pitchers were absolutely dealing. Gord scattered three hits and a walk through his seven innings of work. He had three strikeouts at the expense of only eighty-five pitches. His opponent had a much more gaudy stat line: 9K, 1H, 0BB. But they were both unblemished where it mattered most: on the scoreboard.

With one out and one on in the top of the eighth, Picard sat down with his second-year ace. "How are you feeling, Gordie?"

"Great. My arm feels good. I have lots left in the tank."

"You think you can finish this off?"

"No problem, Perry."

The Wolverines were able to scratch a lone run across in the eighth on a sacrifice fly by TJ Jackson. Gord noticed movement in Michigan's bullpen as he jogged out to the mound for the bottom of the inning. Mike Bertram, the Wolverines' closer, began tossing softly.

*Why is Bertram up? I can finish this game myself,* Gord thought. *What is Picard doing?*

His momentary lapse in concentration benefited Oregon State's leadoff man. He jumped all over a lazy, belt-high fastball and hooked it down the left field foul line. The crowd erupted, finally having a reason to cheer. The batter ended up on second base with a leadoff double.

Gord, pissed off at his lack of focus, bore down on the next two hitters and struck them both out looking—their bats never left their shoulders. With the count 1–2 on the fourth batter of the inning, it looked like Gord would be able to extricate himself from a sticky, late game situation.

McLeod called for a curveball to finish off the left-handed swinging Beaver. Unfortunately, the hitter was looking off speed. He held his hands back long enough to muscle a ground ball to the right of second base.

Paul Pena met the ball in plenty of time, but it kicked off the heel of his glove into short right field. The runner, moving on contact, scored easily to tie the game. Oregon State's bench raced out of the dugout to embrace their leadoff hitter. The home crowd unleashed a vigorous roar as their team finally broke through in the tightly knit contest.

*Fuck. That run's on me,* Gord thought. *I lose my focus for one second and the guy rips that double.*

Gord, to the appreciation of his teammates, didn't let the error affect his demeanour. Pena knew that he had made a mistake. He didn't need his pitcher showing him up by waving his arms around or carrying on with other histrionics.

The next batter popped up foul to the right of home plate.

McLeod circled underneath and snagged it easily. He quickly rolled the ball toward the mound and sprinted into the dugout. The rest of Michigan's defense followed suit. They wanted to get that run back in the top of the ninth.

Pena, due up fourth, approached Gord on his way to the bat rack. "Sorry, Gord. I should have had that one."

"Don't worry about it, pal," Gord replied, slapping his teammate on the back. "Just get me a hit."

On the mound, Oregon State's ace was beginning to tire. His fastball had lost some of its pop and the Wolverines took full advantage.

The first two batters reached on sharply hit singles up the middle. That chased the Beavers' starter. A reliever was brought in to face Jeremy McLeod. Everyone in the park expected a bunt, and Oregon State's defence adjusted accordingly.

The pitcher delivered a high fastball at the upper limit of the strike zone, hoping to entice a popup from the freshman. McLeod was able to get the ball on the ground, but he bunted it too hard, right back at the pitcher, who fielded it cleanly and threw it quickly to third base for the force out.

The third baseman, aware that McLeod was not fleet of foot, took the throw from his pitcher and rifled a frozen rope to first base. Oregon's burly first baseman stretched out and received the throw a full step before McLeod reached the bag. Double play.

Shoulders slumped throughout Michigan's dugout. What had looked like a big inning was now poised to be an opportunity squandered. Now, Michigan only had a runner on second base with two out.

Up stepped Paul Pena. Small in stature but big in heart, Pena looked to avenge his blunder from the previous inning. Overeager, the Wolverines' leadoff hitter quickly fell behind 0–2, as he chased two pitches well out of the zone.

The raucous Oregon State fans rose in unison as Michigan was down to their final strike. John Sukrage, the Wolverines' veteran left fielder, danced off second base. With two out, he would be running on contact.

Pena called time and stepped out of the batter's box. He choked up on his bat and moved a half step closer to the mound.

The pitcher unleashed a tight slider to the outside corner. Pena stayed with the pitch and sliced it through the hole between first and second base. Oregon State's right fielder charged toward the ball and came up throwing.

Sukrage wheeled around third base and headed for home. The fielder let fly with a bullet toward the plate. Sukrage's feet kicked up a cloud of small turf pebbles alongside the foul line as he churned for the dish. The throw bounced once, which slowed the ball long enough for Sukrage to slide in under the catcher's frantic tag.

SAFE! Michigan was up 2–1.

Amid the wild celebration in the dugout, Perry Picard approached his starting pitcher.

"Gord, we're going to shut you down. Bertram's going in."

"What?" Gord was incredulous. "Why?"

"He's fresh. I want him to get the last three outs."

"How many pitches have I thrown?"

"That doesn't matter." Picard spoke firmly. "I'm making the change. You had a great outing."

"Perry, come on," Gord pleaded. "Let me finish this. It's my game."

"My mind's made up. Take a seat." Picard shook Gord's hand and placed a comforting hand on his shoulder. "Great job, son."

Gord's mind was completely blank. *How can he take me out now? They haven't done anything against me all game.* Gord shook his head. *What a classic case of over-managing. Picard's just trying to put his stamp on the game. He wants to prove how smart he is.*

Gord looked at his catcher. McLeod shrugged his shoulders in confusion.

The inning ended with Michigan still clinging to a one-run lead. Gord stopped Mike Bertram in the dugout. "Finish this baby off, Mike." Gord was still upset at being taken out, but he wasn't going to let his anger show through now. He just wanted the team to come away with a victory.

This was Bertram's first year as closer, and his nervousness showed during warm-ups. His pitches were all over the place. The Oregon State crowd, dejected after losing the lead, was buoyed by the pitching change. Their lineup hadn't been able to solve Gord through eight innings, so they hoped their luck was about to change in the ninth. The fans smelled blood as they watched a shaky Bertram throw his eighth and final warm-up pitch.

The Wolverines' closer walked the first batter of the inning on five pitches. He was moved to second on a sacrifice bunt. Another walk put the winning run on first with one out. The air was slowly let out of the Wolverines' winning tire. Bertram, unable to find a consistent release point, fell behind 3–1 to the Beavers' number five stick.

Not wanting to walk the bases full, he grooved a pitch down the middle. The batter did what he was supposed to do with a belt-high fastball and hammered to straightaway centrefield. The ball slammed into the base of the wall and shot back toward the infield. The runners flew around the bases as Michigan tried in vain to relay the ball home.

Both runners scored, and Oregon State walked away with a 3–2 come-from-behind victory. The crowd exploded in delirium as Gord and the Wolverines were left to contemplate what might have been.

Michigan was unable to rally from such a crushing defeat. The next day, they barely put up a fight in losing 7–2. The season was over. It was a disappointing end to a terrific sophomore campaign for Gord. He had turned another corner in his career. Professional baseball scouts were beginning to take notice of the Wolverines' crafty left-handed ace.

# July 2008

## Orlando, Florida

RIIIIIIIIINNNNNNNNNNNNNGGGGGGGGGG!
RIIIIIIIIINNNNNNNNNNNNNGGGGGGGGGG!
RIIIIIIIIINNNNNNNNNNNNNGGGGGGGGGG!

The shrill, incessant whine of the motel room phone thundered in Gord's eardrums. He turned over, the mattress groaning underneath him. He focused his opened eye on the digital alarm clock. 6:30 a.m.

Gord shot a glance to Danny, sleeping soundly. Although *passed out* may have been a more appropriate term. After his three-hit, seventeen-strikeout gem the night before, Danny tried to drink all of Orange County dry of alcohol in celebration.

Shaking the cobwebs loose from his skull, Gord reluctantly picked up the phone.

"Hello?"

"Johnson."

"What?"

"Mattis? It's Tom Conrad; get me Johnson."

"Oh. Yeah, okay. Just a minute, Skip."

Gord placed the receiver on the end table and gingerly removed himself from the warmth of his bed. He gently shook Danny's shoulders, trying to coax him awake.

"Danny? Danny? Come on, man, get up."

Danny was dead to the world. A tribe of wildebeests could have rumbled through the motel room and he wouldn't have stirred.

Gord went to the bathroom and filled a glass with cold water. With a mischievous grin, he flung the icy contents all over his comatose roommate. Danny jumped up like he had been shocked with a cattle prod. Completely discombobulated and dripping wet, he struggled to orient himself.

"Jesus Christ!" Danny screamed. "What the fuck, man!"

Gord could barely contain his laughter. "Skip's on the phone. He wants to talk to you."

"You're an asshole," Danny panted. "I think my heart's going to explode."

"Nah, you're fine. Here." Gord tossed him the receiver. "I'm going to grab a shower."

"Fuck you." Danny took a couple of deep breaths to calm his racing heart. "Hey, Skip, what's up?"

Gord closed the bathroom door behind him. The last thing he heard before turning on the water was Danny loudly exclaiming, "Really? That's awesome! Thanks, Skip."

After a piping-hot shower, Gord wrapped a towel around his waist and re-entered the room to find a contemplative Danny sitting on the edge of his bed. He had his elbows propped on his knees and his hands under his chin like a poorly conceived version of Rodin's *The Thinker.*

"What did he say?"

Danny hesitated as though he hadn't heard the question.

"Danny?"

He slowly turned toward Gord. A jubilant look was plastered across his face.

"I'm getting called up!" he said excitedly. "They're sending me to Double A. Fuckin' Erie, baby!"

"That's terrific, man!" Gord was genuinely happy for his roommate.

With the way Danny had pitched lately, it was only a matter of time. He would be a great addition to the Erie Sharks.

"Skip said I'll be the first eighteen-year-old pitcher in Erie in over fifteen years. They're flying me to Pennsylvania this afternoon."

"I'm going to miss you, man. Who else is going to bring home drunken bimbos from the bar at three o'clock every morning?"

"I know, eh? Think how much money I'll save not getting fined by you in Kangaroo Court."

"Shit, you're right! That's the team's beer money on road trips."

Gord took a seat across from Danny on one of the old wooden chairs that fit so well with the room's dilapidated motif.

"Best of luck to you up there." Gord turned serious. "But remember, these are professional hitters you'll be pitching against. No more cheap draft pick, cupcake outs at the bottom of lineups. Everyone in Double A can swing a stick."

"I'm not worried," Danny retorted nonchalantly. "They haven't seen stuff like mine before. I'm going to dominate like always. It will be a piece of cake. Plus, with the way I'm throwing, I won't be there for long. It's just a stepping stone."

Danny considered his roommate. "What do you know, anyway? You've never been higher than A ball," he said glibly.

Gord reached across the stained motel carpet and slapped him in the face. Stunned, Danny recoiled slightly and stared at his bigger, stronger teammate.

"What is wrong with—"

"Shut the fuck up. I talk, you listen. Look, I've kept quiet all year because you've been lights out all year. I've ignored the binge drinking, the all-night partying, and all that shit. You want to drink and fuck your way through life, that's fine. I don't care. But when you do that crap the night before you have to pitch . . ." Gord shook his head.

"You're good, there's no denying that. You have the best stuff I've ever seen. But you could be GREAT. Screwing around down here, you could pitch drunk and still throw gems. That won't cut it 'up there.' I wish I could throw like you; I really do. But I can't. I have to work one hundred times harder than you to get one-tenth the results. You're a fucking natural."

Danny sat there, listening with rapt attention. No one had ever spoken to him like this before.

Gord continued his monologue. "I love this game more than anything, and it pisses me off to see someone take it for granted. You're letting your talents go to waste. Guys would kill to have your ability; you use it as a mechanism to get laid. You want to be the best? You want people to tell their grandkids 'I saw Danny Johnson pitch'? Then get your fucking head out of your ass and go get it. Work harder than everyone else. Study hitters. Tinker with your mechanics. Hit the weights. You're good? Get better. Strive for perfection."

Silence engulfed the darkened motel room. Danny stared at his sockless feet. Gord had finished his rant. He watched his roommate carefully, searching to see if his message got through.

Danny looked up, and Gord noticed a change in his eyes. Gone was the look of wide-eyed immaturity and incorrigible cockiness. It was replaced with a steely determination and hardened focus that Gord had never seen before.

"You're right, man." Danny looked appreciatively at his fellow pitcher. "You're absolutely right. Thanks."

"Good."

Gord exhaled slowly, like he had something to add to the weighty discussion. Instead, a broad smile broke out on his face. "Now fuck all this serious shit. You just got promoted! You're on your way to the Show!"

Danny smiled back. "I better start packing." He stood up to collect his things.

"Hey, man." Gord stopped him. "I don't want to see you back down here. Give 'em hell." Gord embraced his young protégé, clapping him on the back.

As the Wildcats prepared for the middle game of a three-game set with the Orlando Buccaneers, it was noticeably quieter in the clubhouse without Danny's gregarious personality. Most of the guys were going to miss their young ace, as Danny always kept the team loose when the pressures of playing professional baseball threatened to crack their resolve.

However, there was one player in particular who was not happy to see Danny promoted—primarily because he believed he should have been called up instead: Tyson Dante.

Dante's irrepressible temper reared its ugly head once word of Danny's promotion trickled throughout the visitor's locker room at the Global Sports Complex. Dante stalked furiously into the manager's office and slammed the door behind him.

"What the fuck is going on here, Tom?"

"What is it, Tyson?"

"I'm hitting .360, leading the league in extra base hits and I don't get called up. You have got to be fucking kidding me. Goddamn it, this is total bullshit!"

Conrad's eyes flashed with anger. "Do not take the Lord's name in vain with me, son. Do you hear me?"

"Yeah, but—"

"No buts. I'm not kidding. I hear that again from you and you'll be stapled to the bench. I don't care how well you're hitting. Are we clear?"

Dante's face was crimson. The rage radiated off of him, but he managed to keep his composure, lest he incur a suspension for conduct detrimental to the team. Dante gritted his teeth at Conrad.

"Yeah, we're clear."

"Good. Look, you're playing great and you're a terrific competitor, but the Sharks had an injury in their starting rotation. A spot opened up, so Johnson was promoted. The front office is aware of your success, but there is a glut of infielders in the organization. Just keep hitting, and once the major league roster is expanded, spots will open up. This is your first year in A ball. Everyone has to pay their dues."

Dante wasn't convinced, but he was forced to agree. "All right," he mumbled.

"Dismissed. Batting practice is in fifteen minutes."

Dante left the office without another word. Still seething, he traversed the visitors' clubhouse. Dante avoided all eye contact with his bemused teammates, who had heard his rant and subsequent scolding at the hands of Lakeland's field boss.

Five steps from his locker, Dante was intercepted by Jeff Merkle.

"Tyson, did you read this article about the top minor league hitters in baseball? I don't see your name, which is weird because—"

Dante turned and glared at Lakeland's Rudy. The pent-up frustration from his failed chat with Tom Conrad exploded out of him.

"FUCK OFF, MERKLE!"

The Wildcats' winning ways continued that afternoon, as they found themselves up 8–1 on the Buccaneers after seven innings. Dante led the way with three hits. Each time he reached base, he stared into the dugout for an extra beat, in a childish and misguided attempt to stick it to his manager.

Gord had entered the game in the bottom of the sixth. Conrad wanted him to go once through the order in his latest audition to solidify his berth on the team. The first two innings had gone by without incident. In fact, Gord had shut the door on the Buccaneers pretty soundly, tossing two perfect innings.

However, the rest of the lineup got a pretty good read on Gord's stuff from the dugout. They were poised to jump all over Gord and his pedestrian repertoire in the bottom of the eighth.

To survive in pro baseball, Gord had to live on the corners. Throwing pitches over the middle of the plate was a recipe for disaster. Through his first two innings, Gord had nibbled on the black very effectively.

His third inning was a different story. It wasn't clear if the umpire subconsciously tightened his strike zone or Gord lost some of his sharpness, but the Buccaneers pounded on Gord like a prize-fighter in a brawl against a stumbling drunk.

Balls rocketed all over the Global Sports Complex. By the time the dust settled, Gord had given up five earned runs and seven hits in his final inning.

He was left in for so long because Steve Anderson was scheduled to pitch next, and Conrad was wary to insert Anderson into the game in the middle of an inning. Gord's outing would have been worse, but the Wildcats' infield turned a miraculous double play on a sharp liner to bring the eighth inning to a close.

Gord walked slowly off the mound. He could feel the eyes of the Wildcats' coaching staff boring holes into him as he descended the concrete dugout steps. How could an outing that had started so promising end so badly? Gord had felt good, but he was unable to fool hitters for any substantial length of time.

Since being challenged by Conrad to earn his place on the team, Gord's results had meandered from average to awful. And this was in A ball, where he should have been able to outsmart inexperienced hitters.

Was he washed up at twenty-four? If he didn't turn things around soon, that would become a stark reality.

After the game, which the Wildcats won 8–6, Gord, Steve Anderson, JR Coltrane, and Chris Seaboard went out for a quiet dinner at Davidson's Prime Steak and Lobster in Winter Park. Davidson's was the destination of choice among visiting ballplayers looking for prime cuts of beef.

The purpose of the meal was to celebrate the promotion of Danny Johnson, which was ironic, considering Danny would never set foot in a place like Davidson's because the waitresses didn't wear miniskirts, and wine was the preferred libation of choice instead of tequila shots.

The conversation revolved primarily around Danny's off-field exploits. To Gord, this seemed like a conscious decision by his teammates, as they knew his string of poor performances weighed heavily on his mind. But Gord was thankful for the reprieve. He just wanted to enjoy his dinner and forgot about the turmoil wreaking havoc on his baseball life.

An impressive array of appetizers was set before the hungry Wildcats: black tiger shrimp, deep-fried green beans, and mussels bathed in melted butter.

Coltrane, crunching on a deep-fried green bean, reminisced with his favourite Johnson story. "Remember his first road trip? We were in Clearwater. We didn't really know him that well. Gord, you brought him out to the pitchers' dinner."

"Oh, yeah," Gord recalled, smiling. "How could I forget?"

"We snuck him into the bar; we must have been there for five minutes, tops. No one knew anything about him, just that he threw gas. I'm standing at the bar with him and this bleach blonde tramp in a short skirt and thigh-high boots came up to us."

Their server returned to refill their wineglasses with the house red. Coltrane stopped his story and waited until she left to check on their steaks. He gave a quick glance around the restaurant to ensure no patrons were within earshot.

"She rubbed her ass in his crotch as she moved in front of the bar," Coltrane continued. "He didn't even flinch; ends up buying her a drink. Then he took her out onto the dance floor. It was still early in the night, and the bar was practically empty. She started grinding on him, and I'm pretty sure he had his hands up her skirt. There was still no one else on the dance floor. He might have even lifted her up at one point. It was like watching the Ice Capades." He paused to take a sip of wine.

Gord picked up where Coltrane left off. "Yeah, after ten minutes, he came up to me and asked for the room key. He said he was taking her back to the motel. You have to give the guy credit—he worked fast. I gave him the key but told him he had to leave the cooler of beer outside in the hall for us to drink when we got back."

Anderson piped up. "Yeah, I remember that night. When we got back to the motel, he was in the lobby, in his underwear and with a beer in his hand, trying pick up the front desk clerk."

Seaboard chuckled. "I asked him about it the next day, and he said once he was finished nailing the first girl, he called her a cab but told the cabbie to pick her up at the gas station a quarter-mile down the road. Danny gave her cab money, but made her walk to the gas station because he said, and I quote, 'I had to get rid of her quick because the broad at the front desk was giving me the eye, and I didn't want this chick hanging around salting my game.'"

The table erupted in laughter at Johnson's complete lack of humility and willingness to do whatever it took to get laid. He was a character even by minor league baseball standards.

The steaks arrived, and the conversation all but ceased as the Wildcats focused on devouring their perfectly marbled, thick-cut New York strip loins. Gord raised his hand to signal their waitress to refill their glasses. He suddenly dropped his hand to his side and stared intently across the restaurant.

"What are you looking at, Gordo?" Anderson inquired.

Gord remained silent, completely transfixed on the unknown object of his attention. Anderson followed his gaze across the sparsely lit steak house. The rest of the table followed suit. They saw her at once. She emerged from the opposite end of the restaurant and walked toward a table to the Wildcats' left. She shone like a twinkling star in the never-ending blackness of the night sky.

Coltrane let out a low whistle. "Wow, she is smoking hot. Nice catch, Gordo."

"Hot" did not do this woman justice. Gorgeous was more appropriate. She was statuesque, tall and athletic, with wavy blonde hair that appeared to shimmer in the candlelight. She wore a blindingly white cocktail dress, which, set against her tanned skin, gave her an almost angelic appearance.

Seaboard piped up. "Stop staring and make a move. She's out of your league, but still, it's worth a shot."

Gord looked down and pinched the middle of his brow with his thumb and forefinger. "I know her."

"Bullshit!" Seaboard retorted.

Gord looked back toward Kim. She stopped at a table occupied by an older gentleman with snow-white hair. Her father, Jim. Kim greeted him warmly with a kiss on the cheek and sat down across from him.

"Too bad, Gordo. Looks like she's already got a sugar daddy," Coltrane teased.

Gord exhaled sharply and met the eyes of his disbelieving teammates. "That's her dad. Her name is Kim. We went to Michigan together. She was one of my best friends."

"Then go talk to her," Anderson encouraged.

"I—I can't. I haven't seen her in three years."

"Who cares? Just go over and say hello. You're a pro ballplayer, man. She'll love it."

"She doesn't care about shit like that." Gord was flustered. "I would, but it's just—things didn't end well."

"What happened?"

Gord saw Kim laughing, probably at one of her dad's goofy jokes. He saw the way her face scrunched up, her dimples cutely accented, and old feelings started to well up inside of him. He hadn't thought about Kim for some time, but seeing her again brought back a myriad of repressed memories.

Gord drifted back to the second semester of his third year: the turning point in his relationship with Kim. It was a period of time he looked back on with deep regret, at the loss of what could have been.

# January 2005

## University of Michigan

"Hey, Gordo!"

Gord looked up from his biomechanics textbook and saw the cherubic face of Allan Lysyk, one of Gord's closest non-baseball friends at college. They had lived on the same floor in first year and remained good friends. They bonded over a mutual love of sports, specifically baseball, although Lysyk was a terrible athlete.

Gord was a fan of the game because he lived and breathed it. Lysyk had never played baseball in his life, yet was just as fanatical about the sport. Gord was in love with the romanticized notion of baseball as America's pastime. He appreciated the nuances that made the game so fascinating. On the other hand, Lysyk was a math major. He loved the scientific approach to the analytics of the game through the billion-dollar industry known as fantasy sports.

Gord never understood the draw of fantasy sports. Spending hours poring over mundane statistics and picking different combinations of players to earn the infantile glory of winning a fantasy sports championship was not Gord's idea of fun. He would much rather play than watch.

Gord could not understand how someone could be so passionate about a game without ever having played it. How could Lysyk truly appreciate the game without first-hand knowledge?

Gord considered himself to be a casual fan of professional football but, having never played the sport, he would never be a hardcore fanatic nor have the audacity to question a player's ability over a blown play, which Lysyk did every time one of the guys on his fantasy roster struck out.

In freshman year, Gord and Lysyk sometimes commandeered the residence hall television to watch baseball. Without fail, Gord would be focused on the pitchers' mechanics, the hitters' swings, and defensive alignments, while Lysyk would be huddled with his laptop calculating weird statistics like VORP[4] and adjusted ERA.

"Hey, buddy! How was your Christmas break?" Gord sat at a table on the first floor of the University of Michigan's cavernous Shapiro Undergraduate Library.

"It was good. Nice and relaxed. Yours?"

"No complaints. It was just me and Pops, as always."

"Yeah? How was that?"

"Well, he told me that I better not rest on the laurels of last year's success. He said I should work even harder this off-season to prove last year wasn't a fluke. I think that was his way of telling me that I pitched well last year."

Michael Mattis had attended every Michigan home baseball game over the past two years. Always clad in a blue and gold Wolverines' sweater, he was as familiar in the stands as the team mascot. Their relationship, while still fraught with difficulty, had improved since Gord's transformation from a pitching afterthought to the ace of his college staff.

Lysyk changed the subject. "Did you hear the news about Kim?"

"Nope." Gord jotted down a few notes on a loose sheet of paper. He had a quiz on the muscles of the posterior chain the next day.

"She's single now." Lysyk grinned cheekily.

"What?" Gord stopped writing and stared intently at his friend.

"Yep. Broke up with her boyfriend over the holidays."

"Who told you?"

"Christie." Kim's roommate from first year.

"Really?"

"This is your chance, man. Go for it." Lysyk knew all about Gord's infatuation with Kim.

"I should—I mean I guess there's nothing stopping me now."

"You haven't talked to her yet?"

Gord shook his head. "Not since I've been back."

A whirlwind of emotions flew through Gord. *So much for studying,* he thought. What was his next move? *She's probably going through a tough time. I'm better off being her friend right now.*

Surprisingly, Kim dealt with the breakup quite well. Although she and her boyfriend had been high school sweethearts, they had grown apart, which was typical of long-distance college relation-

4 VORP = Value over Replacement Player.

ships. In fact, she seemed to relish the opportunity to "see what else was out there." Kim began exploring the University of Michigan nightlife much more than when she was in a committed relationship. This only provided an additional level of confusion to her friendship with Gord.

Gord noticed a change in Kim's demeanour when she saw him hitting on other girls. Previously, she had dismissed his casual hookups and teased him about his predilection for sleeping with attractive girls devoid of any personality or intelligence. However, now single, Kim appeared to harbour feelings of jealousy whenever Gord paid attention to other girls in her presence. One such instance took place at the beginning of February, just before Gord left for training camp in Florida.

The majority of their floor mates from first year had gathered together to celebrate Allan Lysyk's birthday. They met at the Hangar on Main Street, which was just a short hop from the campus. Their floor reunions were always raucous affairs and a great opportunity for everyone to catch up and release some steam before midterm exams.

Gord was at the main bar talking to a couple of friends when he noticed an attractive, buxom brunette making eye contact with him from the periphery of the dance floor. She sashayed in front of him on her way to the bar to order a drink. As she walked past, Gord spied a heart-shaped tattoo on her right hip.

Gord nudged his buddies. "Bingo. Target acquired."

Gord confidently positioned himself beside the brunette. He put his elbows on the bar and leaned into her.

"I'll bet I get served before you."

She looked at him and smiled. "You're on."

"What are you getting?"

"Vodka 7. You?"

"Jack and Coke."

Gord made an elaborate attempt to puff out his chest in order to be noticed by the bartender first. Laughing, the girl made the same gesture, except she stood on her tiptoes, leaned over the bar, and displayed her ample cleavage.

Immediately, the male bartender noticed her assets from the other end of the bar and hurried to take her order.

"Nice move," Gord nodded, conceding defeat.

"What can I get you?" the bartender inquired.

"Vodka 7 for me, and a Jack and Coke . . ." she looked at Gord and flashed him a winning smile, "for my loser friend."

"No problem." The bartender left to mix the drinks.

"Loser friend?" Gord feigned indignation. "Harsh, but true. I'm Gord."

"Linda. Nice to meet you. What do I win?"

"An invitation to terrorize the dance floor?"

"Lead the way."

Drinks in hand, Gord led Linda down the steps to the dance floor. He gave his buddies a look to say, *piece of cake*. They nodded back approvingly.

Saturday night at the Hangar was the bar of choice for Michigan's undergraduate students, and tonight was no exception. The place was packed. The dance floor was set down from the main bar area and ringed with five-foot-high partitions. It resembled a rudimentary holding pen.

Most bars had an open-concept dance floor, which allowed excess dancers to spill over into the bar area. Unfortunately, the Hangar was not most bars. The walled enclosure and sunken space gave the students the appearance of sardines stacked tightly in a tin can.

Because of the sheer volume of people, Gord and his new friend weren't able to dance so much as they swayed to the pulsating music in a three-foot radius. Gord had his free arm draped around Linda's tailbone and pulled her close to him. She had her left arm wrapped around Gord's neck as they tried to converse over the dance beat blasting out of the club's sound system.

As their glasses emptied, Gord and Linda began to dance more suggestively, letting their hands explore each other's bodies. She manoeuvred Gord through a tight pocket of open space and pushed him up against the railing at the back corner of the dance floor.

Linda ran her hands down Gord's chest and felt the contours of his core. She turned around, shoved her sculpted ass into his crotch and grinded against him. Gord clasped his hands against her hips as their bodies moved rhythmically together. He bent down and kissed the perspiring skin on her collarbone. Linda shuddered in appreciation.

Gord glanced up and saw a figure stride purposefully toward them. It was Kim. An odd smile played across her face. As she approached, Gord noticed that her eyes were glassy and her cheeks were fire-engine red.

"What are you doing, Gord?" she queried with an accusatory tone.

"What do you mean?" he replied quizzically. "I'm dancing."

"I go to the bathroom and you start dancing with some girl."

She motioned haphazardly to an oblivious Linda. Kim was obviously drunk; her coherent speech was belied by her wobbly gait.

"Why wouldn't I dance?" Gord didn't understand what Kim was driving at. "What's wrong with you?"

Kim ignored his questions and focused her attention on Linda. With her feet shoulder width apart and her hands resting on her hips, Kim sized up her shorter rival.

"Why are you dancing with him?" she sneered.

Linda quickly stepped away from Gord. "Is this your girlfriend?"

Gord turned toward Linda. "No. She's not. She's just a frien—"

"Yes, I am his girlfriend. So you better take your skanky hands off of him before I knock you out!"

"Whatever. Bitch." Linda disappeared into the dancing throng.

Gord was completely speechless. He wanted to coerce Linda to come back, but the words weren't there. The last two minutes had just floored him. Gord turned to Kim, searching for an explanation. She just smiled at him, turned on her heel, and worked her way through the crowd back to the bar. Gord was left standing alone, bewildered by the dumbfounding sequence of events.

Kim had completely destroyed his chances of hooking up with Linda. Not willing to let her get away with it, Gord stalked off the dance floor to confront her. He saw Kim talking and laughing with her first-year roommate, Christie. It was evident Kim was telling her what had transpired.

Christie saw Gord approach first. Her laughter abruptly ceased and was replaced by a sheepish smile. She quickly warned Kim and made herself scarce, not wanting to interfere with the impending verbal collision.

Kim greeted Gord with a doe-eyed, innocent look on her face. Gord threw his palms to the ceiling and leaned in to speak over the deafening roar in the club.

"Kim, what the hell was that?"

Her voice dripped with sarcasm. "I didn't do anything."

"Bullshit!" Gord spat back at her.

"It's not my fault you couldn't close the deal."

"You've been trying to cockblock me all semester. It's starting to piss me off."

"So you don't sleep with some whore tonight. Oh, no, the world is going to end!"

"That's not the point. It's none of your business." Gord paused. "Why do you suddenly care so much if I do?"

Kim was silent as she contemplated Gord's question.

"Well, Kim?" Gord wanted an answer. "You'd only care that I'm with other girls if you wanted me for yourself." He pressed on. "Is that it? Is that what you want?"

Kim was caught off guard. *He's right*, she thought. That's exactly what she was doing. Her feelings had always been there, but, during her relationship, she had always repressed them. Now single, Kim realized that she wanted to be with Gord but she didn't know how to verbalize it.

*Did he still feel the same way?* Drunk and in a bar was not where she wanted this conversation to take place. Instead, she decided to say nothing. In an attempt to mask her true intentions, Kim deflected Gord's probing questions with humour.

She laughed. "Don't flatter yourself, Gord."

He shook his head. "I don't believe you."

"Whatever. Why don't you go find your tramp-stamped friend?"

"Yeah," he replied, disappointed. "Maybe I will."

Gord left Kim and went to the bar to get a drink. He was angry at the non-resolution of their conversation. He'd hoped Kim would express romantic feelings for him. That didn't happen, so Gord figured that liberal amounts of whiskey would wash away his disappointment.

# May 2005

## University of Michigan

"Kim, come out tonight." Gord cradled his cell phone in his ear as he dressed.

"I don't know, Gord," she replied from the loveseat in her living room.

"Come on. The guys won't stay out after the team dinner and I don't want to be at the bar by myself."

The next afternoon, the Wolverines were scheduled to face the Purdue Boilermakers in the first game of the conference tournament. A team dinner had been planned at the Blue and Gold Pub to give the guys an opportunity to relax and clear their minds before the game.

After the meal, the majority of the team would retire to their respective houses to rest and get a good night's sleep. Staying at home was the last thing Gord wanted to do. He had the ball in Game 1, and, his desire to stay at the bar notwithstanding, it was not an assignment he took lightly.

Without question, Gord was now Michigan's ace. He had built on his first taste of college success the year before and unfurled a season that left imprints all over the Wolverines' record books. Ten wins, one loss, and a dominating stat line: 100IP, 77H, 15BB, 79K and a 1.34 ERA.

He wasn't trying to recruit Kim for a night of drunken debauchery that would result in a debilitating hangover the next morning. In fact, in Gord's mind, staying out would actually help prepare him for his start.

Gord always needed to go out for a beer on the eve of his pitching appearances. Otherwise, he would just be cooped up at home, with his mind racing in anticipation. He also knew that the sooner he fell asleep, the sooner the dream would captivate his consciousness. It was not something he looked forward to—he tried to delay that moment as long as possible.

If he was in bed by midnight, Gord could guarantee himself about nine hours of sleep and then head to the park. It was his pre-start ritual. Most of the time, he could coerce one or two guys to join him, but, with the conference tournament looming, everyone planned to head home after dinner.

Therefore, Gord decided to ask Kim to join him. Yes, their relationship had hit a rocky patch at the Hangar three months earlier. In fact, the week before Gord left for training camp, they didn't speak at all, nor for the entire duration of Michigan's southern swing. But, they had smoothed things over and their friendship was back to normal.

"Well, if you're going to be a big baby about it, I guess I'll come out with you."

"Sweet. Thanks, Kim."

"You have to come pick me up, though. I'm not walking to the bar by myself."

"Are all of your housemates gone already?"

"Yep. Julie was the last one and she left last night."

Final examinations had finished that week, so there was a mass exodus of students leaving Ann Arbor. Kim had remained behind due to her job commitments at the campus bookstore. She planned to head back to Orlando on the first of June.

"I'll come pick you up—no problem. Dinner shouldn't take too long. I'll get you around nine?"

"Sounds good. See you then."

"'Bye, Kim."

The Wolverines were scattered around the private party room at the Blue and Gold Pub. Some guys played pool, others played foosball, but the majority of the team was focused on the projection screen TV, which showed Detroit versus Minnesota in an early season divisional showdown.

Gord looked around the room. He noticed Ben Daniels, a freshman pitcher from Virginia, standing at the bar alone watching the game.

Daniels had just finished a rookie campaign worse than Gord's two years earlier. At least Gord got the opportunity to fail in his first year. Daniels had blown a four-run lead in his lone appearance during Michigan's spring training trip and had not appeared in a game since. The benching was so disastrous to his confidence that Daniels couldn't even throw strikes or get hitters out in simulated games during practice.

With first-hand knowledge of such failure, Gord stood up from his seat in front of the TV and approached his teammate.

"Benny, how's it going?"

"Not bad." Daniels ordered another beer from the bartender. "God knows I'm not getting off the bench tomorrow, and with you starting, no other pitcher will either, so I figured I might as well get hammered."

"Hey, I wouldn't blame you. It's tough sitting on the bench watching your team play without you. Trust me, I know."

"You do?" Daniels was unconvinced.

"I do, buddy. More than you'd know. I was terrible in my first year. Most guys are. In my three years at Michigan, I've yet to see a true freshman succeed in his rookie season. It's a tough adjustment going from high school to college."

"Tell me about it," Daniels nodded. "I was the MVP of my high school team."

"You've got a good arm. You'll figure it out."

The bartender returned with Daniels's beer.

"Here, let me get that," Gord offered, sliding a ten dollar bill across the bar.

"Thanks, Gord."

"No problem. Can I give you some advice?"

"Sure."

"I'm going to let you in on a secret for success. And not just success at pitching or sports, but success in life. Have you ever heard of Derek Northcutt?"

Daniels recognized the name. "Didn't he used to play here?"

"Yep. He was a senior during my rookie year. The guy just *looked* like a pitcher, big and strong, and he could throw forever. He never got tired. He had elbow surgery the year before I got to school, so he had lost some of his pop, but he could still bring it in the mid-eighties. Derek was the most mentally tough person I have ever met in my life. Nothing fazed him when he was on the hill. I never saw him get rattled once the entire year: not if guys made errors, not if the umpire squeezed him behind the dish, and definitely not if the offence couldn't score him any runs."

Gord paused briefly to order himself another drink.

"Derek was the epitome of a workhorse. He wanted the ball in every situation against the best teams and the best hitters. If he lost or had a bad outing, he wanted to pitch again the next day to redeem himself. He started, he relieved, and he closed. Northcutt did it all."

"Wow."

"Near the end of the season, I went up to him after practice one day. I asked him what his secret was—what gave him such a commanding presence on the mound."

Daniels was intrigued. "What did he say?"

"Confidence. Derek told me that the most important thing a pitcher needs is confidence. It doesn't matter how hard you throw, or how much control you have, or how good your curveball is; it all starts between the ears."

"That's great, but how I do get that confidence?"

"You have to believe in yourself, Ben. If you don't think you can succeed, why would anyone else think you could? You have to be selfish; you need to be your number one fan. If your teammates see that you're willing to dig in and battle through adversity, then they'll get behind you. They'll believe in you, too. Don't stand on the mound and be scared of good hitters. Fuck them—they should be scared of you. Attack them like they're nobodies. They can't hit you. Think you're better than your opponents. Don't give them any credit."

Daniels liked what he was hearing. "I never thought of it that way before."

"Neither did I. Sure, it may seem egotistical, but who gives a shit. You want to succeed? You need to be self-serving. Confidence breeds success. The moment you lose faith in yourself, you're toast. When you can stand tall after baseball or life or whatever has been shitting on you, and you still come back for more? That's confidence."

Gord replicated Derek Northcutt's speech verbatim. He had committed the talk to memory and recited it to himself any time his own confidence waned.

"You cannot be scared to fail. You have to relish the opportunity to try again. Give it your best shot. Don't make excuses; take responsibility and make it happen. This is not just about baseball. It applies to life as well. You're nervous about speaking in front of a class? You're smarter than everyone else in the room. You're scared to approach a girl at the bar? She's lucky that you want to talk to her. This is the mindset you need to have to succeed. But, most importantly, internalize it. Don't be a loudmouth prick. Tell yourself you're the best, but let your actions determine if that's true."

A procession of waitresses emerged from the kitchen bearing huge platters of food for the hungry Wolverines.

"Thanks for the advice, Gord."

"No problem, Benny." He clapped Daniels on the back. "We pitchers have to stick together. Let's go eat."

After the meal, the owner of the Blue and Gold Pub, and a staunch Michigan athletic supporter, had a surprise for the team as they settled the rather imposing bill.

"Guys," began Farhad Karzhani, a Pakistani by birth and American by choice, "you know you are my favourite team at UM. But only because Michigan doesn't have a cricket team yet."

The Wolverines laughed loudly at the recurring joke.

"This dinner is on the house," he continued. "My gift to you. Now, go kick some Purdue ass tomorrow!" he cried in heavily accented English.

Whoops and cheers broke out among the Wolverines, grateful for the benevolence of the mustachioed Karzhani. One by one, each player went to shake his hand in thanks. Gord approached at the end of the queue and Karzhani clasped his hand warmly.

"Pitch good tomorrow, Gord." He winked. "Bowl me a gem."

"Yes, sir," Gord replied, smiling.

"Okay, boys, who's sticking around for a pint or two?" Gord inquired of his teammates milling around the Blue and Gold Pub's front entrance.

"I don't know, Gord. I think you're on your own tonight, buddy," said TJ Jackson, speaking on behalf of the team.

Jackson's comment was met with nods of agreement from the rest of the Wolverines.

Gord was unperturbed. "No problem, guys. A friend of mine said she'd come out with me for a bit."

"I'll stay for a drink, Gordo," piped up Jeremy McLeod.

"Nice!" Gord exclaimed, draping his right arm across his personal catcher's shoulders. "I knew I could count on my battery mate."

Brent McPhee, the lone member of the coaching staff invited to the dinner, overheard the sequence of events and came over feigning concern.

"Yeah that's what we need: our starting pitcher and catcher out drinking the night before the game," McPhee quipped sarcastically. "I'm sure Perry would love to hear this."

"Come on, Brent," Gord replied. "You used to be cool when you played. We'll embrace our inner Cinderella tonight. In bed by midnight."

"Sure. Have fun, boys. You better be lights out tomorrow, Gord."

McLeod and Gord picked Kim up at her house, and the three of them decided to check out Whisky Commons. McLeod, though a terrific catcher and Michigan's field general on the diamond, was very shy and reserved around the opposite sex.

Gord had informed Kim of his catcher's timidity, and she took it upon herself to include McLeod in the conversation as much as possible. She asked questions about his life, what he was studying, what he liked to do for fun, et cetera. It helped that Kim was never at a loss for words to make small talk.

Actually, it got to the point where Gord must have looked like a third wheel, so deeply enthralled Kim and McLeod were in conversation. Gord didn't mind. Frankly, he was just happy to be out of the house and not thinking about tomorrow's start.

Around eleven o'clock, the three of them decided to call it a night. McLeod lived just off Main Street, about three blocks south of Whisky Commons. Kim and Gord said their goodbyes to the bashful catcher at a deserted cross street. Gord and McLeod exchanged handshakes, while Kim moved in for a hug. The smile plastered across McLeod's face after his embrace with Kim could have powered the street lights along Main Street.

Gord and Kim continued south toward her house. They walked in lockstep, making chit-chat, when Kim asked a question that would prove to have major ramifications on their friendship and, ultimately, lead to its dissolution.

"Do you mind if I crash at your place?"

Gord raised his eyebrows in surprise. “Uh, sure.”

“I hate sleeping at my place by myself. It creeps me out to be there alone at night.”

“You are such a wuss.”

“Shut up.”

Gord laughed. “Yeah, you can stay at my place. But I have to be at the park by noon.”

# May 2005

## University of Michigan

At Gord's house, Kim requested a pair of boxer shorts and a T-shirt so she wouldn't have to sleep in her jeans. She went into the bathroom to change, while Gord stayed in his room.

He was shirtless and wearing a pair of plaid pyjama pants when Kim returned. She gazed admiringly at his body. Unbeknownst to Gord, she had an ulterior motive in her request to spend the night.

"I'm staying in your room, by the way. I am not sleeping on a couch," she stated matter-of-factly.

Now Gord was confused. "Umm, okay."

Was Kim just staying as a friend or were there romantic connotations in her request? He stared at her. Even in a loose-fitting T-shirt, the mesmerizing shape of her body left him speechless.

Kim had finally realized that she wanted them to be more than platonic friends. It was something she had subconsciously known since they met in freshman year, but she had always looked for a way to ignore those feelings. Now, Kim wanted to take their friendship to the next level. Tonight.

Her lame excuse about not wanting to spend the night alone had been technically true, but it was all part of her master plan. Kim assumed that vocalizing her desire to stay with Gord would indirectly give him the go-ahead to act on his romantic feelings.

Gord hesitated as he watched Kim climb into his bed. This was something he had dreamed about for years and it was finally about to happen. Or was it? He had already twice given Kim an opportunity to share similar sentiments, and twice she had rebuffed him.

Did she actually want him to make a move or did she just want some company for the night? Confused, Gord climbed into bed beside her. The anxiety and nervousness he felt at that moment was unlike anything he had ever experienced while in bed with a woman.

They just lay there in the dark. Kim was on her side, facing away from him. Gord was flat on his back, with his hands folded across his stomach. He stared blankly at the ceiling.

"Your room is freezing," Kim shuddered, pulling the blankets up tight around her neck. "Spoon me."

"What?"

She turned to face him. "Have you ever just slept with a girl and not actually had sex? You know, just spooned with her."

Gord pondered her question. "Actually, no. Usually, I leave right after we're finished, or if she's here, I gently suggest that she leave before the sun comes up. You know, keep things casual."

Kim shook her head dismissively. "You're an idiot—time to grow up."

"You have such sweet pillow talk."

"Give me your arm," she demanded.

Kim grabbed Gord's left arm and draped it over the covers across her body. She then rotated her body away from him and pulled him close. Now they were both on their sides, their bodies intertwined.

"This is spooning," she declared mockingly. "Welcome to adulthood."

Gord smiled in the darkness. "Thanks."

He had never been so close to Kim before, in such an intimate setting. His face was inches from her hair. He inhaled deeply. The faint scent of citrus shampoo, mixed with the intoxicating aroma of Kim's perfume, dominated his nasal cavity and left him lightheaded. *Christ, she even smells gorgeous*, Gord thought.

Kim's chest heaved slightly, which mirrored her shallow breathing. Gord, his chest tense, came to an anxiety-inducing conclusion: if he ever wanted to be with Kim, this was his opportunity.

Gord raised his head slightly and looked at her. She looked so beautiful and content lying there with her eyes closed, the faint wisp of a smile playing across her face.

*I should kiss her*, Gord reasoned. *Where? On her collarbone? Would she be receptive?* His mind raced with uncertainty. *Does she want me to make a move? I think she wants me to; that's why she's staying here. What if she doesn't? God, I wish I could read her mind. What is she thinking?*

Kim was thinking, *What is taking him so long?* She ached for him to make a move. After three years, she realized Gord was the one she wanted to be with. But what if he didn't want her? What if he wanted to keep dating floozies and troll bars looking for random hookups? Kim wasn't prepared to lay her feelings on the table. It had to come from Gord. She had to know that he wanted something more with her.

Gord's head pounded as his internal struggle continued. *If I try something, she'll just think I'm looking for sex or that I'm trying something shady. She doesn't even think of me that way. Does she? This could jeopardize our friendship. I don't want to her to think that I just want to have sex with her. I care about her so much. I don't want this to be a one-time thing. I want to be with her. I—I love . . . I love her.*

The declaration blindsided Gord, but it also gave him a newfound clarity. *I love her. I love Kim. Tell her, Gord. Tell her how you feel.* All of the jokes and laughs they had shared over the years, all of the silly conversations and how much fun they'd had together—it had been right there in front of him the whole time. He had always loved her, but he had never truly understood how he felt until now.

*I'm going to tell her*, Gord told himself.

Then, a terrifying thought entered his mind. *What if she doesn't say it back? What if I say it and there's silence in her reply. I can't deal with that. I'll be crushed. Heartbroken. Fuck it, I'm telling her. Screw the consequences.*

Gord cleared his throat. "Kim?"

"Yes?" she replied expectantly.

"I, uh, just wanted to tell you that . . ." SAY IT! TELL HER HOW YOU FEEL! "That, uh, I . . ."

She opened her eyes and looked back at him. "Tell me what, Gord? You can tell me anything."

His heart raced. It felt like it was going to burst out of his chest. Panic paralyzed his muscles.

"I just wanted to tell you that . . ." Gord dipped his head in disappointment. He couldn't pull the trigger. "I set the alarm for nine o'clock."

"Oh. Okay." Kim's face masked her discontent.

She turned and imperceptibly inched away from him. He noticed. He flopped down against the mattress and stared at the ceiling. Gord was appalled at his cowardice. *You are such a pussy*, he scolded. *You blew it.* He stared at that ceiling for hours. He didn't remember falling asleep.

*He's powerless to stop it. The crowd's taunts become more derisive and vitriolic. The boos thunder down onto the field and rattle Gord's eardrums.*

*The walks and runs pile up like stacks of cordwood. Gord looks in desperation to the bullpen, longing for relief and an end to the nightmare, but no one is there. He is completely and utterly alone . . .*

Once again, the dream jolted Gord awake. His body was covered in a thin coating of cold sweat. He groggily turned toward his alarm clock. 5:45 a.m. The morning sun had not yet begun to peek through the plastic blinds covering the bedroom window.

He noticed movement out of the corner of his sleep-encrusted eyes. Kim was gingerly trying to extricate herself from the covers without waking him. She tiptoed across the room, gathering her things. She wanted to leave before the shrill cry of the alarm clock woke them both.

"Kim?"

She stopped abruptly and felt her face flush with embarrassment. "Oh, uh, hey, Gord. I was going to take off. I didn't want to wake you. I figured you needed to rest up for the game."

Gord was silent. He knew she was leaving only to avoid the cringe-inducing awkwardness of the previous night. The tension in the air was palpable. Something had changed between them. Gord's hesitation to declare his feelings had catalyzed a seismic shift in their relationship.

"Uh, thanks." He made a feeble attempt to end the maddening silence. "Are you sure you don't want me to walk you home?"

"No," Kim replied a little too quickly and forcefully. "Just stay in bed. I'll be fine."

A nod was all Gord could muster in return.

Kim hurried to the bathroom to change. Gord was left to ponder the biggest non-decision he had ever made in his young life. He sat up in his bed and held his head in his hands. *Why didn't I tell her?* He kicked himself. *I can't tell her now. That was my only shot and I fucked up. I've lost her as a possible girlfriend. Have I lost her as a friend as well?*

Kim appeared in the doorway and dropped his clothes on the threshold. Their eyes locked. They both knew. Things weren't the same anymore. Last night had been the tipping point in their friendship. They had two choices: become romantically involved or stop spending time together. There was no middle ground.

The silence was excruciating. So many thoughts ran through both of their heads. Each had wasted so many opportunities to tell the other how they felt, but it was never the "right time." And now it was over.

"'Bye, Gord."

"Goodbye, Kim."

That afternoon, Gord pitched with a heavy heart. He threw well, 7IP, 3ER, 7H, 2BB, and 5K, but it wasn't enough, as the Wolverines' offence could muster only a single run in the fourth inning. Michigan never made it out of the conference tournament, and Gord's junior season ended with a whimper.

Gord and Kim never spoke again after that fateful morning. She went back to Orlando the next week and didn't return for her senior year.

Gord heard from some mutual friends that Kim had accepted an on-air position with a local television station in Orlando. Thus, there wasn't a need to return for a fourth year at Michigan. He couldn't help but wonder if he had been a factor in her decision not to return to school.

It would have been weird to bump into each other when the emotional wounds were still fresh. Gord eventually got over his feelings, but he was an emotional wreck for quite some time after that night.

Time did heal all wounds. And for Gord and Kim, it had been three long years of zero contact. It seemed like a lifetime ago. Was anything still there?

# July 2008

## Orlando, Florida

Gord was shocked to see Kim for the first time since the spring of 2005. His steak was left half-eaten on his plate; his appetite had vanished.

His teammates looked at each other quizzically. They had never seen Gord so rattled before. He looked like he had just seen a ghost. They were surprised at how candidly he explained his past with Kim. Emotional conversations about unrequited love were not the bailiwick of professional athletes. An uncomfortable tension hung over their table.

Chris Seaboard attempted to infuse some humour into the situation.

"Gordo, that was a real sweet story. But why don't you grow a pair and go talk to her? It feels like I'm out to dinner with my girlfriend right now."

Gord ignored his friend's barbs, but deep down, he knew that Seaboard was right.

"Yeah, man, you pussied out big time back then. Time to man up," added Steve Anderson.

"She probably doesn't even remember me," Gord reasoned unconvincingly.

"Well, there's only one way to find out. Go over there and talk to her." Seaboard smirked at a reluctant Gord. "If she doesn't remember you, then the resulting awkwardness will at least provide us with the night's entertainment."

"You'll kick yourself if you don't take the chance," said Anderson.

"Here's your shot," piped up JR Coltrane. "The old man's going to the bathroom. He probably has a prostate the size of a watermelon, so he'll be in there awhile."

Gord inhaled deeply. He put his hands on the crisp, linen tablecloth and propelled himself to a standing position.

"You guys are dickheads." Gord paused, adjusting the collar of his dress shirt. *Be a man,* he told himself. "Okay, fuck it. Here goes nothing."

Gord moved slowly toward Kim's table. His heart palpitated ferociously. Each step thundered throughout his body and echoed in his ears. He could feel beads of nervous sweat drip down his back. He wiped his clammy hands on the front of his pants.

Gord's mind searched for an opening line. What could he say?

*Hey, remember me? We used to be best friends and then we stopped talking because I was too much of a chickenshit to tell you how I felt. I haven't seen you in three years. How have you been?*

Gord stopped five feet from her table. Kim was too busy texting on her phone to notice him standing behind her. He cleared his throat. *Moment of truth.*

"Hi, Kim."

Instantly, her hands stopped typing. Kim raised her head slightly, trying to place the voice. A second later, her back tightened and her shoulders rolled back into a position of perfect posture. She knew who was standing behind her.

Kim turned around slowly, as though she was unsure what she would find at her back. Gord had a sly smile on his face as she turned. He lifted his eyebrows as if to say, *Yeah, it's really me.* Bewilderment ran across Kim's face.

An interminable silence passed. She blinked a number of times and shook her head, trying to wrap her mind around the scene. Gord broke out into a big grin as he looked at her up close for the first time in over three years. *She is so beautiful,* he thought.

"Oh my God! Gord!" she exclaimed.

Kim stood up and closed the gap between them. Their joy at seeing each other was quickly replaced by the history of their last meeting. They both moved in for a hug, but instead of a warm embrace, it resembled an awkward greeting between two distant acquaintances. Their arms were wrapped around each other, but their waists were miles apart.

Gord began to speak. "Kim, you look—"

"What are you doing here?" Kim inquired, interrupting him.

"Oh, well, I'm just out for dinner with my teammates."

"Teammates?"

"Yeah. I play ball for the Lakeland Wildcats. Detroit's Single A farm team."

"Really? That's great!" Kim replied excitedly. "You got drafted after school?"

"No, I didn't even get a sniff," Gord shook his head. "Not one scout approached me during my senior year—it was pretty disappointing. I had good numbers, too, but I guess teams didn't think I threw hard enough." He shrugged. "Story of my life."

"I'm sorry to hear that. So, how did you end up with the Wildcats?"

"The Michigan coaching staff set up some independent league tryouts for me after graduation. I threw really well at an open showcase in Illinois and got signed. I went 8–1 with a low ERA in indy ball and the Wildcats signed me at the end of the summer. They sent me to Lakeland for the last month of the season, and I'm back there again this year."

"I'm really glad you stuck with it and followed your dream." She smiled. "I always knew how important baseball was to you."

"Thanks, Kim."

"I heard you guys had a really good senior year?"

"Yeah, it was awesome. After four years, everything finally came together. We made it all the way to the College Championships. Such an unbelievable experience. You should have been there."

Gord's last sentence was more scathing than he intended. He had simply meant that Kim would have enjoyed the spirited atmosphere on campus during the Wolverines' run to the finals. Instead, his comment was laced with disappointment and anger over Kim's departure from school after junior year. He immediately regretted his brief loss of composure. His face flushed. Gord struggled to smooth over his gaffe.

"So, uh," he laughed nervously. "Last I heard you were doing some TV work?"

"Yeah, I'm a features reporter for Channel 13. I do entertainment: celebrity gossip, restaurants, local events, dating. Stuff like that."

Gord grinned. "Hard-hitting journalism at its best, eh?"

"Shut up," she laughed. "I can tell you haven't gotten any funnier."

"Kim, who's this?" Jim Bell had returned from the bathroom.

"This is Gord Mattis, Dad. We went to Michigan together. We lived in the same hall."

"The ballplayer?"

"Yes, sir," Gord replied.

Jim grabbed Gord's right hand and pumped it furiously. "How are you doing, son?"

"I'm great. I just noticed Kim from across the restaurant and thought I would stop by and say hello."

"Why don't you join us?" Jim offered.

"I'd like to, sir, but I'm here with some friends and I should be heading back. Thanks anyway."

Gord turned to Kim. "It was great seeing you, Kim."

"You too, Gord."

They didn't hug goodbye, but instead exchanged warm smiles. Their eyes lingered on each other for just a fraction of a second before Gord turned and walked back to his table.

A rush of mixed emotions wracked Gord. He was happy to have seen her, but old feelings started crawling back to the surface. She seemed surprised, but happy to see him.

*Shit*, Gord thought. *Should I have asked for her number?*

When he returned to the table, the guys looked at him expectantly. Gord felt lightheaded. The last ten minutes had been a blur. He needed some fresh air to clear his mind. What had started off as a low-key celebration for a promoted teammate had turned into an emotionally exhausting night.

Seaboard spoke up first. "How did it go?"

"It was, uh, good." Gord grabbed his wallet from his back pocket. "I'm going to take off, though. You guys stay." He threw some cash down on the table. "This should cover my share. I'll see you guys at the park tomorrow."

Gord left the restaurant without giving his surprised teammates a chance to respond.

# May 2007

## Joliet, Illinois
## Silverback Field

"After you've registered for the tryout, all players are to report to the third base dugout to await further instructions. Have your release forms ready when you approach the desk and remember the number that we give you. That is how you will be referred to for the duration of the tryout."

Gord stood in a long line winding along the concrete concourse encircling Silverback Field. It was just after eight o'clock in the morning, and there were dozens of players waiting to register for the Joliet Lumberjacks' open tryout. The line was moving with the efficiency of the DMV on a weekday morning.

A man clad in a Lumberjacks polo shirt had just addressed the line, hoping the next part of the process would go more smoothly than the initial registration. The team had requested that all players wishing to attend the tryout register in advance, but a huge influx of men chasing their dream had shown up at the field that morning, their $100 fees in hand.

The Lumberjacks, an independent franchise in the Pioneer League, were not going to turn away players with cash, so the registration ground to a halt as the people running the administrative portion of the tryout scrambled to handle the increased demand.

Gord glanced at the varied array of colours blanketing the shirts and hats of the players in front and behind him in line. It was a veritable rainbow of college athletics—it seemed that every colour in the visible spectrum was represented. To pass the time, Gord tried to guess the school of those closest to him in line by the colour swatches, but he quickly gave up.

He'd never heard of most of the schools, let alone knew they had a college baseball program. He did recognize a few players from Michigan's conference, but the rest of the guys were a blur of blues, reds, greens, and blacks.

Gord heard the clang of the steel staircase to his right and looked toward the source of the sound. Wobbling up the steps—in a pair of comically high heels—was a girl in a cleavage-baring shirt and white shorts that barely concealed her ass. She walked beside a player—most likely her boyfriend—and carefully navigated the steep staircase leading to the concourse.

Gord and the rest of players in the vicinity immediately forgot about the numbing wait to approach the registration desk and were transfixed by the sight. They were not expecting to see such a show near the field today. Baseball was immediately pushed from their minds.

The tall, lanky player in front of Gord whistled appreciatively under his breath. He and Gord exchanged bemused glances.

"Jesus Christ, it's way too early in the morning for that," the whistler said.

"Tell me about it," Gord replied. "Do you think she realizes it's only sixty-five degrees out?" he asked, as a stiff breeze whipped through the concourse.

"Better for us," the tall player quipped.

"Welcome to Silverback Field. My name is Chris Carlucci, and I'm the owner of the Lumberjacks."

Carlucci was on the crest of fifty years old, evidenced by his paunch and his balding hairline. He stood in front of the dugout, clutching a list of the names of the players in attendance.

Well over one hundred players looking for a roster spot sat clustered in the dugout and spilled into the first row of seats along third base. They all sat in rapt attention as Carlucci spoke, as he was one of many men they would have to impress to obtain a contract.

"Our goal from today's tryout is to get as many of you guys jobs as we can. Last year we had twenty-five guys signed to independent league contracts. You're not just trying out for the Lumberjacks. There are," Carlucci waved his hand at the men spread out behind him, "representatives from other teams in the Pioneer League, the Border League, and the National Association."

Carlucci let his words sink in to the assembled players as they gazed at the myriad of scouts and directors of player personnel flanking the owner of the Joliet franchise.

"The biggest piece of advice I can give to you today is to leave everything on the field," Carlucci continued. "Don't walk anywhere. Show us you want to be here and that you deserve a contract. I cannot stress that enough. Besides talent, we will be looking for guys who want to work hard. If you're a hitter, then swing the bat. We can't tell what type of player you are from walks. You're here to swing. Pitchers, throw strikes. Challenge batters. Don't nibble on the corners. Play good, hard, smart baseball. We're on your side—we want to get you all signed if we can.

"I want to introduce all of you to the man who will be running the tryout. He's been a special adviser to a number of big-league clubs and he's been in baseball longer than most of us have been alive." He pointed to a diminutive, frail man clad in a Lumberjacks uniform with a thick mane of white peeking out from underneath his baseball cap. "This is Buck Chamberlain. Any of you who harbour dreams of playing in the Show, then this is the guy you want to impress. Take it away, Buck."

Chamberlain limped toward the dugout railing and extended a bony hand toward Carlucci. The Lumberjacks owner shook it and quickly retreated to the group of scouts milling around the on-deck circle. Chamberlain leaned against the railing and stuffed both hands in his back pockets. A giant wad of chewing tobacco protruded out of his cheek. He spat a wad of dip onto the gravel beneath his feet and studied the faces in front of him.

"All of us are here looking for players. If I see someone I like, I will call the big club and let them know what I saw. I've been doing this for fifty years. I know talent when I see it. The front office trusts my eye. There's a chance one or two of you might even get a contract from me at the end of the day. It's happened before. As Chris said, we need you to show us your stuff. We can't sign you if you don't play well. Simple as that. And if you think that's a lot of pressure, well maybe you're playing the wrong game. Baseball is all about managing pressure. If you can't take the heat at a tryout camp with two dozen people watching, then you have no chance playing in front of 30,000 screaming fans."

Chamberlain paced in front of the dugout, his turf shoes crunching over the red gravel. "The itinerary for today: we're going to run you in the sixty-yard dash. We'll give you some time to stretch. After we get your sixty times, you can throw, get your arms loose. We'll do an infield/outfield. After I/O, I want the catchers at home plate. You'll be throwing to second; we need your POP times. Then we'll play an intra-squad game until we see everyone hit a couple of times. Pitchers, none of this applies to you. I don't know what the hell you guys do anyway. Just remember the number we gave you this morning and you'll be throwing in that order in the game."

The players laughed nervously at Chamberlain's straightforward approach. He was not the sort of man to be crossed.

"One more thing for you position players. I know a bunch of you think you can play a variety of positions and want to take reps all over the diamond today. Don't do it. Whenever I hear a kid describe himself as a utility player, I automatically assume that means he can't play one position well. If the fate of the universe depended on the result of a baseball game you were starting, where would you play? That's the position I want to see you at today. A utility player is just another word for a guy who plays like horseshit. Understood?"

Dozens of heads nodded.

"Okay, let's get after it."

For the rest of the morning, Gord and the rest of the pitchers—with nothing else to do—were forced to watch the position players run, field, and throw in the hot Illinois sun under the watchful gazes of Buck Chamberlain and the rest of the scouts.

Gord—taking refuge in the shaded confines of the dugout—wasn't particularly impressed with the talent of the position players in attendance. A good number of them seemed to be nothing more than professional tryout players. These were guys who, every summer, earmarked a couple of hundred dollars of disposable income toward throwing their baseball gear into the trunk of a car and attending every open independent league tryout in a 200-mile vicinity.

They had zero chance of actually obtaining a contract, but just relished the opportunity to play baseball in a professional environment for a day. No one really had a problem with their attending workouts. The teams running the showcases saw the dreamers as dollar signs filling their coffers, and other players looked at them like injured gazelles languishing on an African plain. They were cannon fodder to make a serious player look good. If the dreamer was a pitcher, then hitters jockeyed for the chance to feast on their slow, meaty fastballs and looping breaking pitches. If the tryout player was a hitter, pitchers immediately recognized their weak swing and exploited their terrible plate discipline for a devastating strikeout.

However, there were definitely a couple of players at the tryout who had pro potential, and the scouts took notice, calling a select few fielders over to chat for a few minutes to find out more information about their baseball backgrounds.

As the sun reached its zenith in the sky, the first portion of the tryout mercifully came to a close as the last catcher completed his throws to second base. The grounds crew worked to prepare the field for the intra-squad game as the first pitcher scheduled to throw warmed up in the bullpen.

The pitchers' numbers were organized in alphabetical order, so Gord would throw in the middle of the pack. He hadn't even changed out of his running shoes—there was no need. Each pitcher would throw twenty-five pitches in the game, and then a new arm would be called in from the bullpen. Gord still had a couple of hours to kill before he would take the mound.

"Next pitcher!" Chris Carlucci shouted from behind the batting cage set up behind home plate to collect foul balls.

The other scouts stood around the semicircle of netting with their elbows propped up on the aluminum beams of the cage. Some held radar guns to clock pitch speed, while others charted notes on clipboards. Gord knelt next to the cage waiting for the man on the mound to finish his outing. He was the next hurler. Gord was about to jog out to the hill when Buck Chamberlain emerged wearily from his steel chair near the first base dugout and halted the tryout.

"Hold on a minute, Chris. I want to say something. Bring everyone to the mound."

Chamberlain shuffled toward the centre of the diamond as Carlucci signalled all players to join the grizzled baseball veteran on the hill. Gord jogged toward the mound with a quizzical look on his face.

*What does he want? And why now? I'm warmed up and ready to go.* Gord took a knee at the base of the mound with the rest of the players. Chamberlain stood atop the hill and surveyed his charges like an army general studying a new batch of recruits.

"Men," Chamberlain began, "some of you are giving a good effort, and we appreciate that. But there are an alarming number of you guys going through the motions out here. I don't know what kind of ball you've played in the past, but this is not the way the game is played. This isn't college baseball anymore. We're not here to hold your hands and pat you on the bottom when you make a nice play. This is pro ball, gentlemen. Treat it with respect. The calibre of ball I'm seeing right now should be in a recreation softball game. It's fucking embarrassing." He spat on the ground.

"It's an honour to be on this field. Baseball is the greatest game in the world. It's also a very tough game. You play every day for six months straight. In what other sport are you forced to play so much in such a short period of time? And perform at a high level day in and day out? There's no doubt in my mind that it's the hardest game in the world to play. People always talk about football being a tough sport. Give me a fucking break. Out-of-shape fat guys push each other around for five seconds and then rest for a minute. And they only play once a week. Yeah, real impressive athletes. Football is a joke. Baseball is the sport of kings. Treat it that way."

Gord struggled to focus. There seemed to be no point to Chamberlain's meandering ramblings. Gord broke his gaze from the baseball lifer and stole a quick glance at his fellow players. They had the same bored expression on their faces as he did, marked by constant eye blinking, stifled yawns, and uncomfortable fidgeting from being stuck in a kneeling position. But Chamberlain wasn't finished.

"I couldn't care less about what my players do off the field or during the off-season. I really couldn't. As long as they give me an effort and produce between the white lines, that's all I'm concerned with. Winning baseball games is the number one priority. I told a scout once—he was worried about a prospect's character—I told him I didn't care if the guy was a serial killer in the off-season if he would help the team. I'm dead serious. Now carry yourselves with some fire, some passion, and finish the rest of the day strong. Your careers depend on it. Get back to work."

Chamberlain spun on his heel and trudged back to his folding chair. The players dispersed back to their positions, and Gord climbed atop the mound, shaking the stiffness that had seized his joints during Buck's speech.

*It's about damn time.* His arm had gotten cold. He needed to warm up in a hurry if he wanted a contract.

"Hello? Anyone home?" Gord felt the locking mechanism unhinge as he slid the key card into the slot. He pushed the door open with his right knee. He carefully navigated the doorway as he carried three duffel bags into the room and dropped them onto the linoleum tile.

He heard footsteps off to his left.

"Ah, hello, Bro. What's up?" a Spanish accent floated to Gord from down the hall.

A tall, brown-skinned man with jet-black hair appeared from one of the bedrooms. He was dressed in designer jeans and a dark grey, skin-tight, V-neck T-shirt. He didn't as much walk toward Gord as he seemingly floated toward the open door. The man's hair was coiffed to perfection. He was the epitome of a metrosexual.

"Hey, man," Gord replied. "I guess I'm your new roommate."

"Nice to meet you," he said in heavily accented English. "My name is Yunel."

"Gord." They shook hands. Yunel brought Gord close in a half handshake, half chest bump.

"Position?"

"Pitcher," Gord answered. "I'm a lefty."

"I peetch, too."

"Where are you from?"

"Cuba," Yunel said. "You?"

"Michigan. Do you know where my room is? 112C?"

"Yes, yes." Yunel pointed back toward an open hallway. "Past the TV and around the corner."

"Okay, thanks."

"You need help with the bags?"

"No, I'm good. Thanks, though. We have to be at the park at 2:30 p.m., right?"

"Two and a half, yes."

That afternoon would be Gord's first practice with the Joliet Lumberjacks. He had thrown extraordinarily well during the open tryout: two innings pitched, six strikeouts—it was reminiscent of his first workout with the University of Michigan. After Gord had finished throwing, Carlucci streaked across the field toward him with his hand extended, offering a playing contract with the Lumberjacks. Gord was a member of the Pioneer League before he crossed the foul line. He was by far the best lefty in attendance. His velocity was consistent at eighty-seven miles per hour with pinpoint control, and all of his pitches had plenty of life. It was a terrific performance.

Most independent league teams depended on the generosity of local families to billet players for the summer. Carlucci utilized a different approach to house the team for the season. He struck a deal with Joliet College to put the Lumberjacks in dorm rooms for the duration of the summer. Joliet College had suite-style dorms, which meant four players were housed in each suite. They had their own rooms with a locking door, but the suite also included a furnished living area and a kitchen to prepare meals. Carlucci hoped that placing teammates in close quarters would allow them to jell and bond faster than if the players were spread around town in different homes.

At practice, Gord met the rest of his roommates. They stood in the short grass of the outfield during batting practice getting to know each other.

Dallas Brown was a six-foot-six behemoth from Chapel Hill, North Carolina. He was dark-skinned with a body chiselled out of granite, but his physical appearance belied his cheerful disposition and sunny personality. Brown was always smiling. The third and final roommate was Pierre Coubertin, a French Canadian from the backwoods of Quebec. He was young—still a teenager at nineteen, but looked closer to thirty, and had an abrasive personality that you either found hilarious or ended up wanting to punch him in the face. He had eschewed college to play for the Lumberjacks.

Brown was the Lumberjacks' starting first baseman, while Coubertin was fighting for a starting position in Joliet's outfield.

At Michigan, players were forbidden from socializing during BP; Perry Picard and the rest of the coaching staff believed that batting practice was work time, and players inevitably succumbed to laziness and lacklustre effort if allowed to congregate in small groups when they were supposed to be shagging flies.

Conversely, the Lumberjacks' coaching staff believed that, as long as the pace of BP didn't slow, conversation between players was fine. Plus, it broke up the monotony of batting practice. This was the first foray into the world of professional baseball for most guys, and the Lumberjacks wanted to treat their players like men. They were no longer college boys. And if they wanted to make it to the next level, drive, determination, and knowing when to focus and when to have fun would have to come from within.

Gord wasn't necessarily small by baseball standards, but he was dwarfed standing beside his roommates. They all had big, strong bodies that scouts drooled over. You couldn't teach that kind of size. It was purely the luck of the genetic lottery. Both scouts and front office personnel would give chance after chance to a guy with bowling-ball shoulders, a broad chest, and a lean waist: the superhero physique.

They would ignore a low baseball IQ and less than total mastery of hitting and throwing for the potential to transform athletic freaks into five-tool players. It was a practice with a dismal success rate—and it meant that players with more talent but less physical gifts would be overlooked—but polishing that one raw genetic talent into a once-in-a-generation player with no discernable ceiling made the process worth it in the eyes of baseball men.

"What's the plan for tonight?" Gord asked as a lazy fly ball nestled into the webbing of his glove. "Does Joliet have a good bar scene?"

"Yeah, it's pretty good," Brown replied. "We pretty much run the show here in town. This is my second year with the Lumberjacks. Just stick with me and you'll be all right."

"I love American chicks. They're so much easier than Canadian girls," Coubertin interjected. "I can get any girl I want at the bar here."

Brown laughed. "Shut up, Frenchy. You look like Paul Bunyan with more body hair. No girls at the clubs here want to fuck a gorilla."

Coubertin snorted. "We'll see tonight."

"Goddamit! I can't find my front foot! Where the hell is it?"

Gord and his roommates looked away from the action at home plate toward the bullpen mound near the right field corner. They watched a pitcher kicking violently at the dirt, sending clouds of dust into the air, stammering to himself about his wonky mechanics.

"Who is that?" Gord inquired.

"Billy Nickerson," Brown answered. "He's been on the team forever. He hardly ever plays anymore—he's a complete nut job. I honestly think he's only on the team because Chris and everyone else in the front office are scared he'll try to blow up the ballpark or something if they cut him."

"Bullshit." Gord rolled his eyes.

"I'm serious," the big outfielder said. "Take a look in his eyes when you talk. There's something *off* about him. He has crazy eyes, man."

Gord looked back toward the bullpen. "Is that his fastball?"

Nickerson was throwing to the bullpen catcher, driving hard to the plate with his lower half, but the ball came out uncharacteristically slow. It looked like he was almost shot putting each pitch.

"He's throwing a weighted ball," Brown said.

"From the mound?" Gord was incredulous. "Why the hell would he do that?"

"He thinks it makes him throw faster in games."

"He's going to fuck up his mechanics, not to mention hurt his arm."

"I told you he was crazy."

Gord shook his head. "Apparently."

"He also throws a three-seam fastball," Coubertin piped up. "Ask him to show you some time. It might help your career," he quipped.

There were two main types of fastballs: a two-seamer and a four-seamer. The two-seam was a secondary fastball. It had less velocity than a four-seam but had a downward spin so it appeared to reach the batter waist-high in the middle of the plate before it dove to the bottom of the strike zone. Many pitchers used the two-seam fastball when they needed a ground ball. Conversely, a four-seam fastball was delivered up in the zone. It was the out pitch—pitchers used it to light up the radar gun or when they needed a big strikeout.

There was no such thing as a three-seam fastball unless the pitcher had lost a few fingers in an unfortunate accident.

# May 2007

## Joliet, Illinois

“Fuck, this line is too long,” Gord moaned. “I’m not waiting forty minutes for the chance to drink five-dollar beers.”

Ten members of the Lumberjacks stood outside of Blue Bar, the pre-eminent nightclub in downtown Joliet. Live music blasted out of the front door as the whoops and shouts from the revellers inside drifted through the line huddled on the narrow sidewalk. Those waiting in line eyed the scene just beyond the front door with an intense jealousy.

“We don’t have to wait in line,” Brown stated matter-of-factly.

“What do you mean?” Gord queried.

We play for the Lumberjacks,” Brown said. “No line, no cover. Ever.”

Gord stared at his moon-sized teammate, incredulous that a non-affiliated independent league team carried such weight in the community. He was used to receiving preferential treatment at Michigan, but every varsity athlete at every major program in the country was treated better than the general student population. And minor league affiliates were steps away from the majors, so people went out of their way to please players destined for the Show.

But independent league ball was primarily filled with dreamers and reclamation projects hoping for one last shot at glory. The sad reality was that, in eighteen months, the majority of independent league players would be stuck working nine-to-five jobs they hated, still dreaming of the time when baseball was the only thing that mattered in their lives.

Gord did not want to become another statistic. Indy ball was a means to an end. If he could have a dominating season in the Pioneer League, a pro team might take a chance and sign him to a minor league contract. But he needed a big summer. Gord did not want to be stuck in Joliet next year talking to the new recruits about how much the city loved the Lumberjacks.

Brown walked to the front of the line—with the rest of the team in tow—and spoke quickly with the bouncer manning the front door. The bouncer nodded, stepped aside, and let the players into the club like he was opening the door to Oz, much to the chagrin of the people still in line.

The Lumberjacks sat in a long, curved booth adjacent to the dance floor. Gord sat beside Geoffrey Jackman, Joliet's starting catcher. He was from Canberra, Australia, and in his first year of American baseball. He had destroyed the pitching in the Australian League, hitting over .400 the year before, which was enough for Chris Carlucci to give him a chance against stiffer competition.

However, the conversation was stilted because Jackman kept getting approached by women asking him to dance. He looked like a movie star: dark hair, dark eyes, and a perfect tan. Girls were practically throwing themselves at him, and he barely batted an eyelash. He was used to such treatment. Ironically, Jackman's calm, cool demeanour only made the women want him more. Gord had never seen anything like it. It was like Mick Jagger and Wilt Chamberlain in one supremely tanned package.

The rest of the team—getting barely a sniff from the fairer sex with Jackman's visage at the table—stared with amazement at their fortunate teammate. Yunel was especially flummoxed by the female attention Jackman was receiving. He had just returned from an unsuccessful trip to the dance floor.

"I don't get these girls, here," Yunel said, waving his hand toward the dance floor. "They are different than back home."

"What do you mean?" Gord asked.

"I dance with blonde girl. She very hot. Grinding on me and everything," he cried, getting agitated. "It excite me."

"Excite you?" Jackman queried.

"Yes," Yunel said firmly. "My penis was so wet."

Gord and the Australian burst into hysterics at Yunel's cringingly literal description.

"Why do you laugh?" he asked, his face scrunched in confusion. "I don't understand."

Yunel turned to face Jackman. "It's so easy for you," he moaned. "Girls just love your accent. Why?"

The Cuban looked at a couple of girls eyeing Jackman from the periphery of the dance floor. He proceeded to start a hypothetical conversation with them, his voice barely audible, lost in thumping club music.

"Do you want some beer?" he asked, inflecting his voice with a comically bad Australian accent. "Do you want to go to a party?" He faced Jackman. "That's all you have to say, and the girls want to fuck with you."

"Jesus, that's enough," Gord interjected, covering his face with his hands. "You're embarrassing us."

"Maybe I should get a tattoo," Yunel continued. "American girls like tattoos."

"What would you get?" Jackman was almost afraid to ask.

"Something on my lower back," he said confidently. "Or maybe my front hip. It would look sick, Bro."

"Dude," Jackman laughed. "You can't do that. That's where chicks get tattoos. That's gay, man."

"No, you're kidding," Yunel dismissed his teammate's taunts.

"He's right, Yunel," Gord agreed. "Only girls do that here."

Pierre Coubertin approached the booth on a diagonal, stumbling across the dance floor like a pinball careening off the rails toward his teammates. He was sweating profusely and his eyes were bloodshot.

"How's it going, Frenchy?" Jackman asked.

"I'm such a stud," he slurred. "I've made out with two chicks already. I have better game than anyone here. I bet I can make out with any girl in the bar."

"Really?" Gord challenged.

"Sure," Coubertin shouted, unable to control the volume of his voice.

"Okay, that one," Gord pointed to the next booth. "There."

Their eyes followed Gord's finger. They saw an alluring brunette clad in a sparkling grey dress. She stood with her hands perched strategically on her hips, her back arched ever so slightly. Her mouth was open in a slight pout. She gazed at the dance floor with a disinterested look on her face, surrounded by a group of eight guys who appeared to be in the midst of a birthday party.

"Her?" Coubertin squeaked. Even drunk, he was intimidated by

Grey Dress's icy glare.

"Her," Gord said smugly. "What are you waiting for, Frenchy?"

Coubertin quickly steeled his resolve. "Not a problem," he sniffed. "Watch and learn."

The Canadian veered toward the unsuspecting woman, twice having to stop his momentum so he wouldn't collide with people on the dance floor. He approached on the girl's left and immediately invaded her personal space, lightly spitting on her as he spoke. It was evident that she wanted nothing to do with his drunken pass, but Coubertin's self-awareness had left the premises after his eighth beer.

Gord and Jackman shifted forward in their seats to get a better vantage point of the train wreck. Coubertin's drunken ramblings did nothing to impress the woman. She looked at him with a pained expression. Even Coubertin could tell he was going down in flames. He needed to pull out some heavy artillery.

He leaned forward and planted a kiss on the girl's lips. She recoiled in disgust. Gord and the Aussie howled at the scene. They couldn't believe their teammate had been so brazen. She quickly pushed Coubertin away and slapped him across the cheek, drawing the attention of her table mates.

They all stood up and surrounded the drunk Canadian.

"Oh shit," Gord exclaimed, rising from his seat. He looked at Jackman. "We may have to do something here."

Jackman whistled at their teammates on the dance floor as Gord sprang toward the next table. One of the girl's friends pushed Coubertin hard in the chest. He was knocked backward, his fine motor skills non-existent at this level of intoxication. Coubertin lunged forward as another man crashed a beer bottle into the top of his skull.

Then all hell broke loose.

Coubertin collapsed sideways as shards of broken glass covered the top of his head. A river of blood erupted from the open wound, running over his forehead and pooling into his eyes.

Gord saw the bottle explode on impact and watched Coubertin's legs buckle underneath him. Gord raced toward the coward standing above his incapacitated teammate and speared him, driving his right shoulder into the man's sternum. Gord felt the air whoosh out of the man as they slid across the slick dance floor, a mass of bodies stampeding past them. Before the man could regain his bearings, Gord was on top of him, delivering quick, short strikes to his face, igniting a torrent of blood from his opponent's freshly broken nose.

Though Gord was drunk and high on adrenaline, he was still able to think coherently, despite the mass hysteria of the last few seconds. He punched the man with his right fist, explicitly avoiding any and all contact with his pitching hand. The last thing Gord needed was to break one of the infinitesimally small bones in his wrist or hand in a bar fight, jeopardizing the tenuous grip he had on a professional baseball career. It was the cardinal rule among the pitching fraternity, declared by Kevin Costner's Crash Davis in *Bull Durham*: Never hit a drunk with your pitching hand.

Gord recalled that nugget of wisdom as his left hand was wrapped around the guy's neck. His right hand started to throb after using the coward's face as a punching bag. Gord was just about to release his grasp when he felt a forearm tighten around his neck and drag him onto his back. He was pulled underneath the table in the middle of the booth.

Gord was wrestled to the ground by one of the girl's friends. He quickly scissored his legs, stomping his attacker in the solar plexus, creating some space between them. Gord looked back toward the dance floor and surveyed the scene. Dallas Brown had two guys by the throat, basically goading them to engage him. Gazing at the size of the first baseman, they wisely kept their hands to their sides.

Jackman and Yunel had two other guys wrapped in bear hugs, ensuring that no one else tried to grab a bottle off a nearby table. Other Lumberjacks pushed and shoved with the remaining friends of the Helen of Troy-esque brunette.

Security personnel and Blue Bar bouncers quickly arrived on the scene and began the arduous process of separating the combatants. It was impossible to get an accurate depiction of the events with the blaring bass line pumping out of the sound system and a group of enraged, drunken twenty-somethings screaming at each other.

Security decided the best course of action was to kick both groups out of the bar through separate exits and let cooler heads prevail. They knew Gord's group were members of the Lumberjacks, but didn't want to create any negative publicity for the team, so details of the incident were kept quiet.

Besides some sore knuckles, and seven stitches for Coubertin, the Lumberjacks made it through their first bar fight of the season basically unscathed. Ironically enough, these types of altercations were often team-bonding experiences that brought the guys involved closer together and prepared them for the ups and downs of a months-long baseball season.

"Yeah, Dad, I pitched well."

Gord, his equipment bag slung over his right shoulder, carefully cradled his cell phone in the crook of his neck as he opened the heavy glass door guarding the entrance to the residence hall. It was a few minutes after midnight, and Gord was just returning from his first start of the season for the Joliet Lumberjacks.

It was his first-ever appearance in professional baseball.

The rest of his teammates had returned much earlier, but Gord stayed behind to get his running in after the game. He ran a total of fourteen poles—back and forth along the warning track from the left field line to the right field line. He did this to alleviate the soreness that was sure to follow the next morning.

"I threw seven innings—gave up one earned run, struck out six, only one walk."

"But . . . did the . . . team win?" Michael's voice drifted in and out on the choppy connection.

"Yeah, we won," Gord replied, annoyed that his father quickly skipped over his personal statistics without recognition. "Four–three. I didn't get the decision, though."

"You didn't?" Michael was surprised. "What happened?"

"The reliever in the eighth inning gave up two runs, and then we won it in the bottom of the ninth."

"Were your coaches happy with the way you pitched?"

"Yeah, why wouldn't they be?" Gord was defensive.

"So they're probably going to give you another start?"

"I don't see why not," Gord said. "I mean, I didn't give them a reason not to throw me again."

"Keep working."

"Of course I will. Why would I stop working hard? I'm getting closer to my dream. I had good stuff tonight . . ." Gord let his sentence drift, hoping his dad would step in with a compliment or a morsel of praise.

"Let me know when you pitch next. Get some sleep."

"Uh, okay. 'Bye, Dad."

Gord shook his head, ridding his mind of the doubt that had crept up during his father's interrogation. He trudged up the long staircase toward his dorm room.

A female voice interrupted his thoughts. "Gord?" she called. "It's Gord, right?"

He turned to his right and saw a woman, about thirty years old, sitting at the bank of computers next to the staircase. The light emanating from the monitor and the shadows skipping across the darkened corridor gave her face an eerie glow.

"Yes?" he answered uneasily.

"I'm Cindy," she replied cheerily, standing up from her chair. "I was checking you out on the team roster."

Confusion still played across Gord's face.

"I'm not a stalker or anything," she continued, laughing much too loud.

Gord chuckled nervously.

"How was the game?" Cindy asked.

Suddenly the revelation of who this woman was hit Gord squarely between the eyes. He had heard some of his teammates talk about a woman who hung out at the dorms trying to fraternize with the players. The stories they told seemed far-fetched—Gord had just dismissed them as rumours.

The woman had apparently tried to get the phone numbers of a few players. Some of the younger guys had foolishly complied in the hopes of garnering a late-night booty call. She wasn't ugly, but the amount of craziness apparently swirling around in her head wasn't proportional to her level of attractiveness. Instead of hooking up with the guys, the woman had just bombarded them with odd, cryptic texts at all hours of the night. She left boxes of cereal and cookies outside of their dorm rooms and knocked on their doors in the middle of the night. It had gone from slightly endearing to downright creepy very fast.

*Cindy was the stalker*, Gord realized. He looked around and saw that they were completely alone in the hall.

"Uh, we won," Gord answered cautiously.

"That's great!" Cindy exclaimed.

"Thanks."

"How come you're back so late?"

"What?"

"Well, the rest of the team got back to their dorms a while ago," she stated matter-of-factly. "Why are you just getting back now?"

*Is this girl for real? She must be kidding.* "I was doing my post-game workout," Gord replied, unsure why he had to explain himself to this woman he had just met.

"Oh, okay, just checking." Cindy smiled.

"Well, I better—"

She interrupted Gord before he could extricate himself from the conversation.

"Can I ask you a dorky question?"

"Uh, sure," he replied hesitantly.

"Do you like coffee?"

"What?" Gord was flummoxed by her line of questioning. It was like being cross-examined by a three-year-old. "Do I like coffee?"

"Yes," she chirped.

"Sure, I guess."

"Do you want to go for a coffee?" she inquired enthusiastically.

"Now?"

Cindy nodded happily.

Gord looked at her in astonishment. *This woman is bat-shit crazy.* "I don't think anything is open right now."

"That's true. Silly me."

*Okay, Gordo, you need to get yourself out of this. Nip it in the bud.* "It's probably not a good idea anyway. I'm kind of seeing someone," Gord lied, wanting to let Cindy down easy.

"She could come, too?" she asked hopefully.

He couldn't help but laugh. Cindy didn't take the hint.

"I don't think so," Gord said with finality.

"Have you ever been in love?"

The question floored him. A lump developed in his throat. *What the hell?* Gord found himself thinking about the question. *What's wrong with you? She's crazy. Don't give what she says the time of day.*

Pictures flashed in his mind like eruptions of lightning stabbing the night sky. They were pictures of Kim. He hadn't thought about her in over a year and an innocuous question by a random woman in Illinois caused a boatload of memories to flood his brain. Why was he thinking about Kim? There was nothing between them. She wasn't a part of his life anymore, yet there she was — never far from his mind.

Gord was rattled. He didn't know what to say, what to do. He just left Cindy standing there in the dark as he walked back to his room in a daze. Gord didn't even remember falling asleep that night.

Had he ever been in love?

Yes. He still was.

# August 2008

## Tampa, Florida
## Heroes Field

"Mattis, how's the arm feel?"

"Great, Skip. I have one more in me."

"Good. I'll get Anderson loose for the ninth. You get us there."

Tom Conrad clapped Gord on the shoulder and shuffled to the other end of the dugout. He took his regular perch on the top step of the dugout railing, adjacent to the on-deck circle.

Tristan Beem marched confidently to the plate to lead off for the Wildcats in the top of the eighth. Lakeland led 5–3 against the Tampa Americans, New York's Single A affiliate. Gord gazed around the impressive façade of Heroes Field. It was a scaled replica of the New York's iconic stadium, complete with concrete friezes and large columns that were reminiscent of a miniature Roman Coliseum.

The Wildcats usually "got up" for games against the Tampa Americans more than any other ball club. Especially games at Heroes Field. New York was the team to which all other clubs compared themselves, in terms of on-field success. This had a trickle-down effect in the minor leagues as well. Everyone wanted to beat the Americans.

Gord was doing his part to make that goal a reality. His performance thus far had been terrific: 2IP, 1H, 0R, and 2K. Gord was carving up the Americans' hitters. They couldn't put a solid swing on the ball. The lone hit was a tomahawk chop that dribbled toward third base on a 0–1 curveball. Gord made the Americans hit his pitches and managed to keep them off balance with an array of curveballs and changeups, and a diving, two-seam fastball.

Beem struck out. The second batter of the inning grounded a weakly hit ball back to the pitcher. Two out. Tyson Dante, already with two hits on the day, was up next.

It had been a week since Gord's encounter with Kim at the steak house. He'd found himself with a little more pep in his step over the past seven days. Instead of dwelling on how things had ended between them, Gord reminisced about all their good times. He had forgotten how happy he was when he hung out with Kim.

No woman had ever made him laugh as much as Kim did. Gord noticed that there had been a small spark of that playfulness at the restaurant. Could that continue? He toyed with the idea of calling her at work. What was the worst that could happen?

The sharp crack of the bat jolted Gord back to the present. Dante sent a scorching grounder between second and third base. The shortstop got a great jump and snared the ball on his backhand. He planted his right foot, pivoted his hips toward first base, and threw a missile across the diamond.

Dante started slowly out of the box, anticipating a clean single to left field. When he saw that the shortstop came up with ball, he frantically increased his speed, trying to the beat the throw to the bag. The ball smacked into the first baseman's mitt a split second before Dante's foot hit the base in an explosion of dust and chalk.

The umpire pointed at the bag and theatrically cocked his right fist in the air signaling the inning's third out.

Dante lost it.

He slammed his helmet into the ground and threw his batting gloves toward Lakeland's dugout. The Wildcats' first base coach tried to intercede before Dante could focus his derision on the umpire, but he was too late. Dante lunged at the man in blue. His eyes were wide with fury and a fine spittle of dip dribbled down his chin. Curses streamed out of his mouth like machine-gun fire.

Dante bumped the umpire in the chest as the crowd rained boos down upon him. He made George Brett in the pine tar game look like Jack Nicholson at the end of *One Flew over the Cuckoo's Nest*.

Tom Conrad and the rest of the coaching staff managed to get the crazed Dante under control. He was unceremoniously booted from the game and most likely faced a suspension at the hands of the Central Florida League's disciplinary committee.

The rest of the Wildcats exchanged sideways glances. This would make for an interesting bus ride back to Lakeland. Gord ignored the buzz in the crowd and climbed atop the mound to begin his warm-up pitches.

The Americans' lineup was comprised primarily of Dominican imports. Over the past few years, New York's front office brain trust had made a substantial financial commitment to develop more Caribbean talent. The Tampa Americans were a testament to that monetary outlay.

They were mainly teenagers eager to make an impression on the organizational bigwigs. Therefore, they swung from their asses on every pitch. It was obvious that the Tampa Americans possessed prodigious talent, but they lacked a certain refinement and polish that would come from further seasoning in the minor leagues.

Gord got ahead of the first batter of the eighth. He threw two changeups that corkscrewed the Americans' centrefielder into the red clay of the batter's box. He practically lunged through the zone trying to take a hack at Gord's offerings.

Gord noticed that the hitter was on his tiptoes, standing right on top of the plate. He figured it was time for some hard stuff over the inside corner. Dave Rockwood was on the same page and flashed his pinkie finger, signalling an inside fastball. Manoeuvring his six-foot-three, 225-pound frame toward third base, Rockwood held his mitt an inch off the black.

Gord, throwing with confidence, let fly with an eighty-eight-mile-an-hour fastball.

THWOCK.

The ball nestled neatly into Rockwood's glove. The batter unleashed a meek, defensive swing that missed the ball by a foot. He was completely fooled. One out.

Gord ran the count to 1–2 on Tampa's second hitter. The free-swinging Americans were the type of hitters Gord thrived against. If he could hit his spots, then Gord could take advantage of their overeagerness to hit the ball.

The old axiom, "You don't walk off the island" certainly applied to these Dominican expats. Their desire to succeed in professional baseball was so all-encompassing because they had no backup plan. They had nothing to return to if they failed. This was their livelihood. Their only way to make an impact was to swing. And swing. And swing some more. You didn't make an impact by taking pitches.

At twenty-four, Gord had the maturity to expose such callow weakness. The batter popped out to third base. Gord retired the Americans in order when the third batter of the inning lofted a fly ball to right field on the next pitch.

Gord jogged happily into the Wildcats' dugout and exulted in the congratulations from his teammates. He had just unfurled three shutout innings against Tampa in their home park and had successfully bridged the gap to Steve Anderson.

"Great outing, Mattis," shouted Tom Conrad as Gord walked past. "Way to pitch. That's what I need from you."

Gord nodded appreciatively to his manager and sat down beside Dave Rockwood. "Great sequences, Dave. They had no idea what was coming."

"You pitched great. Lots of confidence. You hit your spots, breaking stuff was sharp. Good velocity on the fastball, too. That's your best outing in a while."

"Thanks. Hopefully I can start stringing together a few more zeroes."

As the ninth inning began, Gord contemplated his recent success. *That's what I have to do every outing,* he thought. *Throw with command, throw with confidence, and trust my pitches. Remember what Northcutt told you.*

Gord figured that he had until the middle of the month to persuade the front office that he was worth keeping around. Would he be able to convince the organization that he was a legitimate prospect, and not just a guy taking a spot from a younger pitcher with a higher ceiling? *Tom will have no choice but to keep me on the staff if I keep throwing like this.*

Anderson had an eventful bottom of the ninth. He gave up one run and loaded the bases with two out. The crowd smelled a comeback, but Anderson ensured that they went home unhappy. He struck out the Americans' number five hitter on a full count with one of his patented heat seekers. The Wildcats won 5–4.

The bus ride back to Lakeland was a happy one, as the win had completed a three-game series sweep for the Wildcats over Tampa. However, one team member was noticeably silent in the revelry. Tyson Dante stewed in his seat with his arms crossed for the entire trip.

The team had fully expected Dante to continue his rant about being robbed of a hit by the "idiot" umpire. His silence meant that the Badger, Tim Reid, had severely reprimanded Dante in the locker room after his childish tirade. Tyson Dante was a complete head case, but he wasn't stupid. He knew better than to cross the intimidating Reid, unless he wanted permanent injury to accompany his forthcoming suspension.

The bus returned to Lakeland just after six o'clock. Gord had the apartment to himself, now that Danny had moved on to greener pastures. He ordered a pizza and sat down at the circular Formica table that doubled as his dining room. He mindlessly flicked through the channels on the television, absent-mindedly stopping at the Channel 13 *Action News* broadcast. *I wonder if Kim's on,* he thought.

He watched until the top of the hour, but did not see Kim flicker across his TV screen. Disappointed, he caught up on the day's sports highlights. He tried to focus on the stories permeating throughout the sports world, but he was distracted. He kept thinking about Kim and their chance meeting the week before.

An idea popped into Gord's head. *Should I? What's the harm? I won't know if I don't try.* He went down to the lobby of his apartment building, which doubled as a weekly rate motel.

Mrs. Henderson, the black octogenarian building manager, manned the front desk lobby just as she had for the better part of half a century. Widowed twenty years earlier, she was still sharp as a tack and loved baseball players.

"Hi Mrs. H. How are you doing tonight?"

"I'm great, hon. Did you boys win today?"

"We did. Five to four. I pitched three shutout innings."

"That's fantastic, Gordon."

"Thanks. Do you have an Orlando area Yellow Pages I can take a look at?"

"I think so. Let me check."

Mrs. Henderson shuffled slowly into the back. The ravages of osteoarthritis had slowed her gait considerably. A few minutes later, she returned bearing two large telephone books.

"Do you want a hand with those?" Gord inquired as she struggled mightily with the massive tomes.

"Don't be silly. I may be an old woman, but I'm not useless," she snapped back at him.

"Yes, ma'am," Gord replied sheepishly.

Dropping the books on the lobby desk with a loud thud, Mrs. Henderson grinned at Gord mischievously. "What do you need these for? Looking for a lady friend?"

Gord smiled back at her. "Something like that."

"I had my fair share of suitors back in my younger days. Especially during spring training. All of the big stars always wanted to take me out for dinner." Mrs. Henderson looked skyward and closed her eyes, as if a reel of her life played inside her eyelids. "I was quite the catch back then."

Gord looked around uncomfortably. Once Mrs. Henderson got started on the "golden age of baseball" in the 1940s and 1950s, she was impossible to stop. She had stories about everyone: Mantle, DiMaggio, Aaron, and Jackie Robinson. And most of her stories were intended for a "mature audience."

"I remember one night: Bob Gibson took me for a ride in his big Studebaker down the coast in Cocoa Beach. He took me in his big, strong arms. The moonlight sparkled in the waves and he—"

Gord gently tried to cut her off. "Uh, Mrs. Henderson, I really should be going. I have to make this call."

"Oh, go ahead. You young people are always in such a hurry. I understand."

Gord smiled, grateful for the reprieve. "I'll bring these back in the morning. Good night, Mrs. H."

"Take your time. 'Night, sugar," she replied warmly, as visions of Bob Gibson frolicked around in her old mind.

Back in his apartment, Gord found the main station number for Channel 13. He dialled and followed the automated prompts into the station's voice-activated directory. Gord confidently said the name "Kim Bell" and waited for a connection to be made.

"Hi, you've reached Kim Bell . . ."

*Damn,* he cursed internally. *The machine.*

"I am in the office from ten to six Monday to Friday. Please leave your name and number, and a brief message, and I'll get back to you as soon I can."

Gord hung up. He wasn't going to fumble through a poorly constructed voicemail message. *Ah well. I'll just try again tomorrow.*

Gord woke at nine o'clock without the assistance of an alarm. This underrated pleasure was due to the Wildcats' having a night game that evening at Mercantile Stadium.

Gord's left arm barked in obvious duress. The three innings he had tossed the day before had left his shoulder and elbow joints cracking and creaking like the floorboards of a century-old home. He went for a light jog to increase the blood flow to his extremities and did a few sets of push-ups and pull-ups to transform the barking in his arm to a mild whimper.

Famished, he stopped off at a greasy spoon for a hearty breakfast. After his plate was all but licked clean, Gord glanced at the clock on the pastel pink wall. Noon. He had to be at the park at two o'clock. He knew he was stalling. He was nervous about calling Kim.

*What is wrong with you? This is getting pathetic. Nut up, for Christ's sake!*

The personal pep talk forced him out of the restaurant and back to his apartment. Gord sat on his bed and stared at the phone.

*Come on, just do it.*

He took a deep breath and punched in the numbers. He waded through the automated system once again. Kim picked up on the second ring.

"Kim Bell."

"Hi, uh, Kim. It's Gord." He held his breath, praying for an enthusiastic greeting.

"Gord! Hi!"

His prayers were answered. "How are you?"

"I'm good. I'm just prepping for today's segments. It's nice to hear from you. What are you up to?"

"Not bad." *Shit, that didn't answer her question.* He tried to maintain a semblance of poise. "I'm heading to the park in a bit. We have a game in Lakeland tonight."

"Cool."

He heard the rustle of papers on the other end of the line. *She was busy. Get to the point.*

"Anyways, Kim, the reason I'm calling is that we have an off-day the day after tomorrow . . ."

*That was true.*

"And our coach always makes the team do these community involvement activities all over the state on our off-days . . ."

*Also true.*

"So we actually have one scheduled in the Orlando area. At the Troubled Teens Shelter, I think . . ."

*False and False.* The team had won ten of their last twelve. Conrad had given the Wildcats the whole day off to do as they please.

"I was wondering if you wanted to grab lunch. Say one o'clock?"

Gord waited with bated breath as Kim pondered his offer.

"Sure. Yeah, I can do that. Where did you have in mind?"

He laughed nervously. "Actually, I hadn't gotten that far yet."

"Okay, let's meet at Glade Restaurant. It's four blocks north of the station at Eola Drive and Church."

"Great. Sounds good," he replied, making a mental note of the restaurant and major intersection.

"Okay, I have to run. See you then, Gord."

"'Bye, Kim."

Paint thinner couldn't peel the megawatt smile off Gord's face. Whistling to himself, he got ready for the short commute to the ballpark. However, baseball was the last thing on his mind. He was more excited for his upcoming lunch with Kim.

# August 2008

## Orlando, Florida

"What can I get you, pal?" the bartender inquired.

"A beer," Gord replied. He glanced around the sparsely populated restaurant. "Lunch rush already been through?"

"Not yet." The bartender checked his watch. "It will start to fill up once the power lunch crowd gets here. In fifteen minutes the place will be jammed."

"Glad I got here early, then." Gord slapped a five dollar bill down on the mahogany bar.

The bartender slid the bottle of beer in front of him. "Here you go."

"Keep the change."

"Cheers."

Gord took a slug of the ice-cold lager. The intense humidity caused a slick film of moisture to form on the outside of the bottle—it looked like it was sweating.

*Good. I'm not the only one*, Gord muttered internally. He wiped his perspiring brow.

The Glade Restaurant staff had decided to forego the building's industrial-strength air conditioning system. Instead, the windows around the dining floor were left open in the hopes of creating a cross-breeze. It worked, but the hot August wind slapped Gord in the face like steam emanating from a blast furnace.

He kept one eye on the door. Over the next few minutes, Gord observed a steady procession of people flow into the restaurant. The tables on the main dining floor quickly filled up, and space at the bar was at a premium. Gord finished his beer and tried to order another.

"How many drinks do you need to get through this lunch?"

He smirked and spun around. "That depends on how boring my company is."

"Always such a gentleman," Kim said sarcastically.

They hugged. A good hug this time. Their bodies clung close together, partly by necessity, as the bar area overflowed with people.

"Sorry I'm late."

"It's okay. I haven't been here long. You look good." Kim wore a form-fitting blouse and a knee-high navy blue skirt.

"Thanks," she smiled. "Where are we sitting?"

"I got us a table on the patio. Follow me."

Gord guided Kim through the crowd, ushering her along with his right hand strategically placed on the small of her back. The patio was quiet and secluded from the main dining area, allowing them to talk without uncomfortably straining across their table.

"How long have you been in Lakeland?" Kim asked after their waitress had taken their drink orders.

"About a year. Detroit signed me out of an independent league team in Joliet, Illinois, last August."

"Will they move you up soon?"

"I haven't pitched that well this year, so that's doubtful. But I've really turned a corner over the last two weeks. I've reeled off ten scoreless innings in my last five outings."

"That's great."

"What about you? You've been at the same station since you left school?"

"Yep. I started off as a runner behind the scenes, but after six months they let me try some small on-air segments. I tested really well, so I've been getting more and more on-camera responsibility."

"Nice. You still living with the folks?"

Kim laughed that infectious chuckle Gord found so endearing. "No! Thank God!" She took a drink of the white wine the waitress had just placed in front of her. "I moved out, uh, July of last year? I bought a condo just off the 408 overlooking Lake Lucerne. On Orange Avenue."

"I have no idea where that is, but it sounds nice."

The elegant presentation in which Glade Restaurant served their fare was destroyed once Gord and Kim dug into their meals. The remnants of Gord's angel hair primavera and Kim's sesame ginger chicken littered their respective plates. They spent the majority of their meal catching up and reminiscing about their university days.

Of course, the trip down memory lane explicitly avoided the unpleasantness of that fateful night three years earlier. Neither Gord nor Kim was ready or willing to address the issues that led to the termination of their friendship.

"Remember in second year, a bunch of us from the floor went out for Alexandra's birthday?" Kim began.

"Is that when we went to that martini bar?" Gord asked, trying to recall the night.

"Yeah, there were about ten of us. I think you and Allan were the only guys."

"Oh, yeah. That was a bad experience."

Kim laughed. "You were in rare form that night. I don't think I've ever seen you so drunk."

"Well, it wasn't my fault. I'd never had a martini before. I thought they were like mixed drinks. I didn't realize they were pure alcohol."

Kim shook her head. "Being an idiot isn't a good excuse," she retorted.

"Hey," Gord pointed his left index finger at Kim for emphasis. "If you girls could have handled your alcohol a little better, I wouldn't have had to finish off everyone's martinis plus my own."

"Whatever you need to tell yourself, big guy. All I know is we had photographic evidence of you passed out on the toilet in the unisex bathroom." Kim laughed loudly at the mental image she just created. She always knew how to put Gord in his place.

"But, the important thing is, I've matured greatly since then," Gord explained, trying to save face.

Kim looked at him unconvinced. "Yeah, I hear all professional baseball players behave with the utmost maturity."

Gord flashed a knowing grin. "Sometimes."

Kim smiled back. The waitress walked over to hard-sell some of Glade Restaurant's renowned dessert options. Gord and Kim both politely declined as the waitress removed their plates and cutlery.

Gord took a deep breath. He had been searching for a way to broach this topic in the natural flow of conversation, but he had been unsuccessful thus far. The suspense was killing him. He had to know.

"So, how's the love life?" he asked nonchalantly. "Is there a Mr. Bell on the horizon?" Gord continued, hoping his cavalier attitude would mask his unrelenting curiosity.

"What love life?" Kim chortled. "I've been way too focused on getting my career off the ground to have a serious relationship. I've dated a few guys here and there, but nothing of great consequence."

Gord remained stoic throughout Kim's answer to his question, but inside he was doing cartwheels. *She's single! This is great news*, he thought. The corners of his mouth desperately wanted to curve up into a broad smile, but Gord managed to keep his composure. *Maybe I can get another shot?*

"Gord?"

"Uh, what? I'm sorry." He had been too busy trying to keep his jubilation under wraps to hear.

"I said, 'What about you?' You know, dating-wise."

"Oh, uh, well, pretty much same as you. The constant travelling makes it tough. Plus, there are certain 'temptations' on the road that don't translate to a committed relationship."

Kim looked at him with a combination of pity and disgust. "You're still whoring your way through life?"

"No, no. Definitely not. I mean I've dated a few girls here and there and met some women in different cities, but I'm not out there looking to hook up every night."

She tilted her head skeptically.

He continued. "I'm serious. I have to live vicariously through the guys right out of high school for that stuff."

"Wow. Maybe you *are* maturing. Little Gordie's growing up," she joked with a condescending tone.

Gord rolled his eyes. "Yeah, thanks."

The waitress returned with their bill. Both Gord and Kim reached for it simultaneously, bumping their hands together in the process.

"I got it, Kim."

"No, no. You don't have to."

"I want to. Lunch was my suggestion. My treat."

"You sure? We can split it."

"Don't worry about it," Gord exclaimed with finality.

He grabbed his wallet out of the back pocket of his shorts, did some quick mental math to calculate the price with tip, and slapped his plastic down on the table.

"Thanks, Gord." Kim checked her watch. "Well, I should really be heading back to the office. I'm just finishing up a story on the perils of Internet dating."

Gord chuckled. "Sounds like fun."

"Oh, it's riveting stuff." Kim smoothed her skirt with her hands and stood up.

Her sharply defined, tanned legs were directly at Gord's eye level. He watched for a split second before standing. His physical attraction to Kim had not lessened at all.

"I had a great time, Gord. Thanks. We should do this again."

Kim took a step toward him and they hugged warmly.

"Absolutely," Gord replied. "Actually, we have a two-game series here on the fifteenth and sixteenth. I'll be pitching in one of those games. Do you want to come watch? I can get you a ticket. It will be just like old times."

Kim considered his offer. "Sure, I'd love to. Give me a call when you know what game you're pitching."

"Awesome," Gord replied. "Have a good day, Kim."

"You too, Gord. 'Bye."

He watched her leave the patio as several pairs of male eyes followed suit. After paying the bill, Gord didn't so much walk out of Glade Restaurant as he floated happily back to his car.

He was going to see Kim again and she was going to watch him pitch. He just hoped his strong performances would continue and he'd be able to show off with Kim in attendance.

# August 2008

## Lakeland, Florida

*The walks and runs pile up like stacks of cordwood. Gord looks in desperation to the bullpen, longing for relief and an end to the nightmare, but no one is there. He is completely and utterly alone . . .*

Gord woke with a start. Sweating profusely, his hair was matted to his forehead. The dream had once again taken hold of his night in its jaws and refused to let go. The cold dampness of his pillow was a tactile reminder of the anxiety the dream caused his body. Gord rolled over to check his nightstand.

Seven o'clock. Gord had to meet the team at the stadium at noon for the bus ride to Orlando for that night's game against the Buccaneers. Conrad had told Gord that he was first out of the bullpen.

Now that he was awake, Gord wasn't going to fall back asleep now. He saw the blinking red light of his cell phone illuminate the darkness on his dresser. The light indicated that he had received a text message while he slept.

He shuffled groggily to his feet and pushed his wet hair back off his forehead. He felt his way across the bedroom. Shaking the cobwebs from his head, his vision cleared, and he peered at the LED display on his phone.

One unread message. It was from Kim.

*Thanks for the update re: tonight. Where do I pick up my ticket? Looking forward to it!*

Gord was grateful for Kim's enthusiasm. He had been worried that she might have made other plans or forgotten about the game entirely. Gord hastily typed a reply.

*Your ticket is at Will Call under your name. Our team has a block of tix. See you tonight!*

Gord sat beside Chris Seaboard on the Wildcats' chartered coach bus to Orlando. Seaboard knew Gord liked to keep to himself on days he pitched, so conversation was kept to a minimum. Gord decided to break protocol and removed his headphone ear buds.

"Remember when we were at dinner at Davidson's a couple weeks back? I saw that girl I knew from college?"

"The blonde in the white dress?" Seaboard asked rhetorically. "Fuck, how could I forget?"

"Yeah. She's going to be at the game tonight. I invited her."

"Really? Nice. Are you nervous?"

"A little bit. I mean she came to watch me pitch at Michigan, but this is a little different. I think this could be my second chance with her."

"Go for it, buddy. But she is way too hot for you," Seaboard teased. "You need to hang onto that *Cliffhanger* style. Don't let go."

Gord laughed and chopped his fellow reliever in the chest. "Thanks for the pep talk, Chris. You're a good friend."

"Hey, if you don't make a move, I might have to." Seaboard looked directly at Gord to emphasize his point. "She's a goddess, man."

With a runner on, Dave Rockwood crushed a sinking liner down the right field line. The Buccaneers' fielder got a great jump on the ball and sprinted toward the foul line in front of Lakeland's bullpen. The relievers had a great view of the action as Orlando's right fielder laid flat out to snare the ball. He caught it just before it bounded off the wide strip of dirt encircling the playing field.

The fielder's large frame slammed into the ground, kicking up a cloud of dirt and chalk, but he somehow managed to hang onto the ball. Lakeland's pitchers had no choice but to grudgingly applaud their opponent for such a spectacular play.

The catch held the game scoreless as the action moved to the home half of the fourth.

In the bullpen, Gord worked through a bag of dill pickle-flavoured sunflower seeds. Steve Anderson plopped down beside him on the bench. Anderson stuck his hand out expectantly.

"Hook me up with a few of those," he demanded.

Gord obliged, and Anderson tossed a few seeds into his mouth.

"Has that blonde shown up yet?" he continued.

"Not sure," Gord answered truthfully. "I can't remember where our block of seats is in this park."

"I think they're behind our dugout," Anderson offered. "Toward home plate?"

Giving their backsides a reprieve from the uncomfortable aluminum bench, they stood up and craned their necks up the foul line toward their dugout. There were just small pockets of people in attendance, but Gord and Anderson were too far away to be able to differentiate individual fans.

The bullpen phone rang, and Tim Reid grabbed it off the receiver. The Badger peered down the length of the dugout until he spotted Gord and Anderson leering into the stands.

"Mattis," Lakeland's gruff second-in-command barked, "Cole's shoulder's a little wonky." He nodded toward the mound and Wildcats starter Chad Cole. "Warm up. You're going in next inning."

For the moment, Gord immediately forgot about Kim. He got his glove, and Aaron Carmack, and headed to the bullpen mound to start throwing.

"Time!" the home plate umpire roared.

At Dave Rockwood's request, the game was momentarily halted. Removing his mask, Rockwood trudged toward the mound.

Gord stepped off the rubber and ran his left hand through his hair. This was not the way he had planned on starting his outing. Gord hit the first batter of the fifth inning and had just walked the second hitter on five pitches. Two on, none out.

Gord was overthrowing, trying to throw the perfect pitch. He was trying too hard because he knew Kim was watching. He had to get his shit together soon, or Orlando was going to turn a scoreless pitchers' duel into a blowout.

"Gordo, what's going on, man?" Rockwood inquired.

"Fuck. I'm trying to strike guys out on one pitch."

"Just relax. Throw like you've been throwing the last two weeks."

Gord exhaled slowly. "You're right. Nice and loose. Pitch to contact."

"Exactly. Hit your spots."

Gord looked at the runners occupying first and second. "Well, I'm not making it easy on myself."

Rockwood lightly punched Gord in the abdomen. "Just get me a ground ball. You've got good 'D' behind you."

Rockwood jogged back behind the plate and signalled for a changeup. He wanted Gord to slow down his delivery and not overthrow.

*Okay, Gord, focus,* he told himself. *Worry about Kim after the game. Focus on pitching right now.* He took the sign and delivered a strike to the lower half of the zone. The batter, taking all the way, watched it go by.

Sticking with the slow stuff, Rockwood called for a curveball. Gord unfurled a beauty, and the hitter chopped a hard hit grounder right at the shortstop. He flipped it to second, who relayed it to first. The runner was out by three steps. Double play.

Emboldened, Gord attacked the next batter and retired him on three pitches. Inning over. Disaster averted, Gord jogged self-assuredly off the mound. His eyes searched the faces in the crowd as he neared the foul line.

Gord squinted through the bright lights illuminating the field. He noticed a figure waving in his direction about twelve rows up the stands. He spied the blonde hair first and then saw Kim's broad smile. He returned the gesture and acknowledged her with a slight tip of the cap before he disappeared into the dugout with his teammates.

The Wildcats were able to scratch a lone run across in the top of the sixth to take the lead, 1–0. Gord skipped out of the dugout for the bottom half of the inning with renewed confidence.

If Gord's first inning was defined by wildness and timidity around the strike zone, then his second inning was defined by a blitzkrieg attack of the plate. He poured in strikes. Inner half; outer half; at the belt; at the knee; slow stuff; hard stuff. Everything clicked. He didn't give the Buccaneers a chance to be selective at the dish. Gord turned them all into free-swingers. He sandwiched three routine ground ball outs between a hard-hit single that buzzed the top of his head.

Tyson Dante, fresh off his eight-game suspension for his crazed tirade in Tampa, smashed a long home run in the top of the seventh to provide Lakeland with a two-run cushion.

In an attempt to disrupt Gord's rhythm, the first batter in the Orlando seventh tried to bunt his way aboard. The Buccaneer pushed a drag bunt toward no man's land on the left side of the mound. Gord bounced off the rubber with cat-like reflexes.

He speared the ball with one hand, whirled around, and delivered a chest-high strike to Drew Allen, the Wildcats' husky first baseman. One out. The infielders rifled the ball around the horn.

Gord felt great on the hill. After a shaky first inning, he had buckled down and returned to recent form. He marvelled at how well he had pitched over his past few appearances. The confluence of command, velocity, mechanics, and confidence was something he hadn't experienced since his summer in Joliet.

The second batter of the inning lofted a lazy fly ball to medium depth in centrefield. Tristan Beem easily camped underneath the can of corn.

Suddenly, Beem thrust his arms into the air. The glare from the bank of lights behind home plate marred his vision. Beem lost the flight path of the ball and stumbled blindly to where he hoped it would land. He miscalculated by twenty-five feet. The ball dropped innocently to the outfield grass.

The Buccaneers' hitter, in an impressive display of hustle, ran hard on contact and managed to make it all the way to third base before Beem heaved the ball back to the infield.

Now, with a runner in scoring position and less than two out, Gord really had to get nasty to keep Orlando off the score sheet. He also wanted to pick up his normally sure-handed centrefielder. To do so, Gord would have to get through the meat of the Buccaneers' lineup.

The number three hitter took two close pitches for balls to start his at-bat. Rockwood shot Gord a look. *Do you want to just put the guy on with an intentional walk?* Gord shook his head emphatically from side to side. He didn't want to put the tying run on base. He wanted to go right after the hitter.

The batter, eager to put his team on the board, was looking dead red. He expected a fastball. The Wildcats' battery decided to use this aggressiveness to their advantage and throw a 2–0 changeup. It was a risky move, but Gord was confident enough in his stuff to try it.

He unleashed a beauty that dove away from the right-handed

hitter's wheelhouse. The batter meekly tapped a grounder to Drew Allen, who played even with the bag. Allen corralled the ball, looked the runner back to third, and stepped on first base for the inning's second out.

Next up was the Central Florida League's home run king and Orlando's cleanup hitter, Bill Bickford. Bickford cut an imposing figure in the batter's box. At six feet six inches tall and a lithe 240 pounds, he didn't have the biggest musculature in the league, but he made up for it with tremendous bat speed.

The velocity at which Bickford's bat travelled through the hitting zone caused the ball to ricochet off his lumber at a different sound frequency than most guys. The majority of hitters made contact with a sharp crack akin to a pistol being fired in the air. Bickford's bat sounded like a stick of TNT exploding in a jail cell.

Gord had first-hand knowledge of that sound. He had also learned that any pitch left down in the zone to Bickford would promptly be deposited into the next county. In two previous at-bats versus Gord, Bickford had a home run and a ground rule double. It didn't matter if the pitch was inside or outside; Bickford's massive reach covered the entire plate.

However, he did seem susceptible to pitches above the belt. Bickford's swing was a little bit too long to handle anything upstairs. Of course, only fastballs could be thrown to that location. No pitcher was dumb enough to hang a curveball to Bickford, unless they wanted to see a batted ball break the sound barrier.

Without a fastball that could touch ninety, Gord's only hope was to bust the behemoth in on his hands. Gord looked out toward the bullpen and saw both Steve Anderson and JR Coltrane warming up. This was Gord's last inning and probably his last batter. He figured he might as well empty what was left in the tank.

He ripped a fastball right above Bickford's hands. Sure enough, the giant swung underneath it and Gord was ahead in the count, 0–1. Two more fastballs and the count was still in Gord's favour, 1–2.

This was a perfect spot for an off-speed pitch well off the plate. It would change Bickford's eye level and hopefully get him to chase something in the dirt. Unfortunately, with a runner on third, neither Gord nor Dave Rockwood was willing to take that chance. Instead, Rockwood extended his index finger to signal a fastball, but he added two other signs to differentiate this pitch from a normal offering.

First, he turned his thumb skyward, like a Roman emperor saving a gladiator from the slaughter, to indicate that he wanted this fastball at the letters. Then, Rockwood curled his fingers into a fist and shook it twice, wanting Gord to reach back for a little something extra.

Gord nodded. With the ball still in his glove, he shook his left arm slightly, like he was cocking the chamber on a handgun. He started his delivery and pulled the trigger. The ball shot toward the plate in a blur of white. Bickford's face lit up as he recognized another fastball. The pitch came in at eye level, which made it all the more enticing for Orlando's cleanup hitter.

But Bickford had no chance. His bat whipped through the zone, missing the pitch completely. The ball smacked into Rockwood's mitt, a full foot above his catcher's mask. Inning over.

Gord pumped his fist as he jumped off the mound. Not only did he preserve the lead and leave a runner stranded at third, but that shutout inning was his fifteenth in a row.

Descending the dugout steps into the warm embrace of his teammates, Gord noticed Kim standing and cheering wildly. This time, he ignored professional decorum and waved at her as he disappeared into the dugout.

# August 2008

## Orlando, Florida
## Global Sports Complex

The mood was festive in the Wildcats' locker room after their 2–0 whitewashing of the Buccaneers. The team was scattered throughout the clubhouse, in various stages of undress, enjoying a few victory beers. With another game in Orlando the next day to complete the two-game set, the Wildcats didn't have to worry about a bus trip on a dark stretch of Florida freeway. They were all looking forward to a night on the town.

Gord avoided the celebration, despite the protestations of his teammates, and managed to shower and change in record time. On his way to the locker room exit, he was stopped by a naked Drew Allen. Dripping wet, Allen had just emerged from the shower, beer in hand.

"Gordo, stay for a few beers," he slurred.

"Can't, buddy. Next time."

"Oh, come on. What else are you going to do?"

"Sorry DA, I can't make this one." Gord clapped Allen on the shoulder and grinned. "I gotta see about a girl."

"You gotta see about—" repeated Allen, struggling to place the quote Gord had just uttered. Suddenly, the light bulb turned on in the first baseman's foggy mind. "Ah, nice one. Okay, Will Hunting, you do what you have to do."

Allen turned back to the escalating celebration. Gord bolted out of the clubhouse toward the players' entrance, which was connected to the auxiliary parking lot at the Global Sports Complex.

The night was warm, but without a trace of humidity. Gord glanced around the parking lot. A few stragglers made their way to their cars, but the area around the players' entrance was noticeably quiet. Hordes of autograph-seeking fans were not a staple of the Central Florida League, unless someone from the majors was rehabbing an injury.

"Mr. Mattis, Mr. Mattis, can I get your autograph?" a female voice called out in the darkness.

Gord looked in the direction of the voice and saw Kim walk toward him, a pen and paper in her hand.

Gord laughed. "Hey, Kim."

He leaned in for a hug, but she stopped him short with a Heisman Trophy-calibre stiff arm.

"I'm serious. Give me your autograph." She thrust the pen and paper toward him.

"Really?"

"Yep."

"Okay." Incredulous, Gord obliged her with a shake of his head.

"Great." She admired his handiwork.

"Do you want to get something to eat?" Gord inquired.

"Sure."

"Where are you parked?"

"Over there." She tilted her head back and to the left.

"Lead the way—I'm starving."

Kim decided to take Gord to the Pomegranate restaurant in downtown Orlando. Located in an urban-chic neighbourhood, Pomegranate was a stylish bridge between the emerging uptown district and the older section of the city.

Kim pulled into the parking garage at the back of the commercial development complex that housed Pomegranate. They made their way from the garage to the street exit and continued around the building.

The atmosphere around Pomegranate was electric. It was just after ten o'clock, and the weekend party crowd had started to build to a crescendo. Dozens of people swarmed the sidewalks on both sides of the street, all dressed to impress.

However, the partiers in pastel-coloured dress shirts and tiny cocktail dresses were heading to the cluster of nightclubs north of the restaurant. This allowed Gord and Kim to duck into Pomegranate and grab a quiet corner table rather easily.

"You pitched really well, Gord," Kim exclaimed as they perused their menus.

"Thanks. I felt great."

"It looked like you were throwing harder than I remember."

"I've been lifting weights. I'm huge now," Gord quipped. He cheekily flexed his bicep at her.

"Oh, God." Kim looked down at her plate, her face flush with embarrassment. "You're such a dork."

Gord laughed. "Seriously, though, it was great having you at the game. It felt like we were back at school. Just like old times."

Kim smiled warmly and glanced at her menu. "What are you getting?"

"I think I'm going to go with the pork tenderloin. You?"

"The seafood bowl."

Gord read the description. "Interesting choice. You're a Florida girl to the end, aren't you?"

"What can I say?"

The conversation flowed easily throughout their meal. Old inside jokes and odd non sequiturs known only to the two of them dominated the evening. If Gord closed his eyes, he could have sworn they were in the East Quad dining hall on the University of Michigan campus, and not hundreds of miles away in a fancy Orlando restaurant.

However, there were bouts of silence that hung through the air at Pomegranate. But these were not awkward, tension-filled moments. Instead, Gord and Kim, as they gazed into each other's eyes across the expanse of white cloth, used these silences to rediscover feelings that had long been dormant.

It wasn't mentioned explicitly, but they both felt a swelling of emotions as the evening progressed. This was acknowledged solely by the exchange of knowing smiles, which appeared and disappeared like a candle flame flickering in the wind.

After dinner, Gord and Kim emerged from the restaurant into the warm breeze meandering across the street.

They walked along the wide pedestrian concourse toward the entrance to the parking garage. Conversation had all but ceased; there was a noticeable gap between them as they walked. They each tried to make sense of the whirlwind of emotions fluttering around them.

They climbed the metal staircase to the second level. The sound of their feet thudding on each step reverberated throughout the tiny stairwell. It was a helpful reprieve from the silence.

Kim stopped on the stairwell landing as Gord continued up the steps. He noticed her absence beside him and turned, looking down at Kim from the middle of the staircase. He watched her. A puzzled look played across her face, like her mind was ploughing through thousands of bits of data, searching for a solution. Kim's eyes narrowed, confusion reigning, lost in thought.

Suddenly, she focused on Gord and her features changed. A supreme vulnerability appeared as Kim stared up at Gord with innocent eyes, desperately wanting to ask a question, but unsure if she wanted to hear the answer. Surprised, Gord opened his mouth to speak, but Kim interrupted, diving headfirst into murky waters.

"Why didn't you make a move?"

"What?"

"When I slept over at your place at the end of third year. Why didn't you make a move?"

"I wasn't sure—"

"I basically threw myself at you. And you did nothing." Kim's emotions surfaced. "That was so embarrassing for me. I thought you wanted to be with me." She blinked through tears and looked at Gord, waiting for an answer.

"Kim, I did. More than anything," he paused, the lament from that night washing over him. "But, I didn't know how to say it. I wasn't sure how you would react."

"What do you mean?" she demanded.

"Well, I'd asked you twice before if there ever was a chance of us being more than friends, and you said no. Both times."

"You're right. I was lying to myself," Kim admitted. "But, in three years, you never showed me you were capable of having a serious relationship. I wasn't going to be just another notch on your bedpost."

*She's right,* Gord realized. *I can't argue with her. I have to make her understand she's the one I've always wanted.*

"Kim," Gord began, "I did play the field more than I should have. But, you have to know that—and this is the absolute truth—every girl I've ever been with, I've tried to compare her to you. And they never did. They still don't."

She considered his words. "It broke my heart that our friendship ended that night. I was really hurt that you never told me how you felt."

"Kim, I've regretted that for so long, you have no idea. I've wanted to be with you since the day I met you. Truthfully, I was scared to tell you how I felt. I was scared to put myself out on a limb like that."

"I wish you would have." Kim shook her head sadly. "We could have had something special," she said wistfully

Gord was buoyed by a sudden surge in confidence. He didn't have the fortitude to do it three years ago, but he realized this was his second chance. A chance to rectify a lost opportunity. A chance to let the woman he loved know how he felt.

"We still can."

Gord moved toward her, bounding down the metal steps. His feet echoed on the landing and he grabbed Kim's face with both hands and kissed her deeply and passionately. In a deserted stairwell in Orlando, Florida, their arms wrapped tightly around each other, Gord and Kim finally succumbed to feelings that each thought were unrequited.

They burst through the front door into Kim's stylish modern condo.

It was adorned with sleek, cream-coloured furniture atop miles and miles of plush, snow-white carpeting. It looked like a scene ripped from the pages of an IKEA catalogue.

Neither Gord nor Kim paid any attention to the interior design of her home. They were completely focused on each other. Gord pushed Kim against the wall of the foyer, rattling the paintings hanging above them. He dug his teeth into the nape of her neck as Kim moaned approvingly.

Kim reached her hands down toward Gord's waist and swiftly snatched his shirt over his head, exposing his naked torso. She ran her fingernails down his abdomen and pulled him close by the waist of his jeans.

Gord's arms were outstretched on either side of Kim, braced against the wall. He moved away from her neck and buried his face into the flesh of Kim's chest, navigating the soft terrain with his tongue.

Giggling, Kim wriggled her way out of Gord's grasp and ducked underneath his right arm. She skipped away into the middle of the living room and turned to face him. With a seductive smile, she curved an index finger toward him in a come-hither motion, inviting

Gord to follow.

He pursued Kim into her bedroom. Rapidly stripping off their few remaining articles of clothing, they fell onto the bed with their mouths locked together.

Hovering above Kim, Gord stared intently into her eyes. This was the moment he had been waiting for. He had given up hope of its ever happening, but the time had finally come. As if reading his mind, Kim smiled, pulled his head toward her, and kissed him deeply. Gord slowly thrust forward. A gasp escaped Kim's lips.

Afterward, Gord and Kim collapsed in a heap of tangled bedsheets and pillows. Their bodies, dripping with perspiration, lay blissfully intertwined as their chests heaved, lungs gasping for air.

"That was amazing," Kim sighed.

"Yeah," was all Gord could muster. He turned on his side to kiss her. "It was definitely worth the wait." He wrapped his arms around Kim and pulled her close.

Gord felt the warm glare of the sun wash over his face. He squinted through clenched eyelids and gazed out the large bay window at the glistening aqua blue and green of Lake Lucerne.

His mind drifted back to the night before. *Did that really happen? Or was it all just a fantastic dream?*

Gord's questions were answered when something stirred on the other side of the bed. He glanced over at the very real form of Kim lying beside him. She was naked, except for a lone bedsheet clinging perilously to her chest.

Gord reached out and massaged the tanned skin of her upper arm. Kim shifted toward him as the sheet fell from across her chest down toward her navel.

"Mmm," she replied throatily. "'Morning."

Gord leaned over and gently kissed her forehead. "Good morning to you, too. Do you know what time it is?"

"Let me check my phone," she answered, propping herself up on her right elbow. Gord gently massaged Kim's shoulders.

"It's nine-fifteen."

He stopped the impromptu massage. "What?"

"Nine-fifteen."

"Shit!" Gord exclaimed, jumping out of bed.

He hunted frantically around the room for his clothes. "I'm supposed to be at the park at ten. We play at one."

"Do you want me to give you a ride?"

"No, it's okay," Gord said, slipping his polo shirt over his head. "You stay and sleep. I'll catch a cab."

Gord ran his fingers through his dishevelled hair and took one last glance around the bedroom, making sure he didn't forget anything.

"I'll give you a call on the bus back to Lakeland."

"Promise?"

"Absolutely," Gord replied. "I lost you once. I'm not doing it again."

"Good answer." She smiled.

"'Bye, Kim." He planted one last kiss on her forehead and slipped quietly out the bedroom door.

Gord could have lifted a mountain. The endorphins and fuzzy feelings of love made him feel invincible. He couldn't remember the last time he had been so happy. Everything in Gord's life had converged perfectly together. On the field, he was pitching the best of his professional career and, off the field, he had finally captured the girl of his dreams.

# August 2008

## Lakeland, Florida
## Mercantile Stadium

Gord, with his feet propped up on a wooden training table, sat shirtless and drenched in sweat in Lakeland's clubhouse. He had just finished an arduous workout in the Wildcats' weight room.

The rest of the team started to trickle into the clubhouse to prepare for that night's contest against the Palm Beach Crabs. Enjoying his last fleeting moments of solitude, Gord pored over the stat sheets posted biweekly on the locker room bulletin board.

It had been ten days since Gord spent the night with Kim. Things couldn't have been better between them. They talked on the phone every day and had even managed to squeeze in two dates, despite their busy schedules.

The week before, the Wildcats played a three-game set versus the Daytona Bears. Coincidentally, Kim had work commitments in the Daytona area at the same time. They were able to meet up after the middle game of the series. Gord and Kim spent the night in his motel room, as a replacement roommate for Danny Johnson had still not been assigned.

Kim had also made a trip to Lakeland to visit Gord when the Wildcats were in the midst of a rare weekend off-day. While their romantic relationship was still in its infancy, Kim and Gord's previous friendship and familiarity with one another had fostered a strong bond between them.

They had the best of both worlds: the sexually charged intimacy of a bourgeoning relationship, and the comfort and stability of a committed partnership. Although the words hadn't been uttered, Kim and Gord were in love.

Smiling, Gord focused his attention back to the stat sheets. He had led Lakeland's entire rotation in ERA over the past fortnight. He stared at the three digits beside his name in the earned run average column and was ecstatic with their numerical symmetry: 0.00. Over the past two weeks, Gord had not allowed an earned run in six appearances, totalling fifteen innings.

This snapshot of his success was part of a larger picture of improved performance over the past month. Since being challenged by Tom Conrad to improve upon his poor early season results, Gord had drastically stepped up his game. He was proud of himself for answering the bell and showing resilience, with his baseball livelihood on the line.

For the year, Gord's numbers were much improved from the first six weeks of the season: 37 innings, 3.93 ERA, 45 Hits, 8 walks, and 23 strikeouts. His batting average against had fallen to a very respectable .267. At first glance, Gord's numbers wouldn't have blown anyone away, but considering where he was six weeks ago, he had put forth a commendable body of work.

"Oh, Christ. Are you gonna frame those?" inquired Chris Seaboard, as he strolled into the clubhouse. "Maybe make a copy and put them on your fridge?"

"Fuck off, Seaboard," Gord laughed. "I can autograph these for you if you'd like. The closest you'll get to three doughnuts in a row like this is during the postgame spread."

"How's it going, buddy?" Seaboard greeted Gord with a mid-level five.

"Can't complain, pal. Things are good," Gord replied. "You on the bump tonight?"

"Yeah, man. Conrad's giving me the emergency start. Cole's shoulder is still sore. Probably from jacking off too much."

"Mattis!" Tim Reid barked over the din of Gord and Seaboard's laughter. "Skip wants to see you in his office."

"Thanks, Coach," Gord replied, as the Badger stalked off to do whatever he did when he wasn't terrifying players.

Gord assumed that Conrad wanted to quickly commend him for his stellar results over the past few weeks. Therefore, he didn't bother putting a shirt on as he made his way to the office of Lakeland's field boss.

He rapped his knuckles on the door frame, indicating his presence. "Skip?"

Conrad took his glasses off and surveyed his left-hander. "Gord, come in."

Gord took two steps into the dingy office and waited for Conrad to deliver a formulaic "Keep up the good work" address.

"Close the door and have a seat."

A chill ran down Gord's spine as he turned to shut the glass door. He looked inquisitively at his manager, hoping Conrad's face would reveal the point of this meeting. But Conrad was stone. A perfect poker face.

He cleared his throat. "Gord, I just wanted to tell you what a great job you've done over the last month. You've been one of my most dependable relievers and are one of the main reasons the club has been playing so well recently."

Gord felt his body relax slightly with each compliment. "Thanks, Tom. I feel like I've really turned a corner here. I'm looking forward to the rest of the season."

Conrad diverted his gaze. He scratched at an imaginary spot on his rusted metal desk.

"I know we had a discussion awhile back about your future with the organization." Conrad's voice wavered slightly as he continued. "I told you that some of our younger arms were breathing down your neck and you needed to prove to the front office that you were worth a spot on the club. And based solely on the numbers, you've done that."

Gord's heart was in his throat. He didn't know where Conrad was going with this speech.

"Unfortunately, this is not just a numbers-based decision."

Gord mustered a faint nod. *What did that mean?* He waited for his manager to explain.

"Our scouting staff has been following each minor league affiliate in a sort of blitzkrieg scouting session. The front office wants a report card and recommendations for advancement of every player in our system. I have your report right here," Conrad said, tapping the impressive stack of papers occupying the right side of his desk.

Gord felt the acidic taste of bile creep up his throat. His mind speculated wildly on what was written in his report.

"Basically, our scouts have determined that your ceiling is A ball." Conrad jumped right into the crux of the report, as though it would lessen the sting of his message. "It has been recommended that your contract be terminated immediately to make room for some pitchers with greater potential." Conrad looked at his left-hander with sad eyes. "And I have no choice but to follow that directive."

The air rushed out of Gord like he'd just had a date with the front end of an express train. *Contract terminated? They're releasing me?* He struggled to make sense of his manager's words.

"If it were up to me, I'd keep you on the roster to help this team win. Unfortunately, you know as well as I do that the minor leagues are in place to develop big league talent, not to make the Central Florida League playoffs."

An uncomfortable silence hung in the air. Gord stared blankly at the floor. *I'm cut? My ceiling is A ball?*

Deep down, Gord knew that he didn't have the stuff to make it to the Show. He had seen the writing on the wall. Watching Danny Johnson pitch for half a season only reiterated as much. But Gord didn't care. So what if he projected to be a career minor leaguer. He just wanted to play baseball for a living. Gord had been proving people wrong at every level since high school. A part of him foolishly hoped that, with enough hard work, he'd be able to do the same in the minors. But he wasn't going to get that chance.

Gord offered a meek point of contention. "But Tom, I haven't given up a run in fifteen innings. I've led the staff in ERA the past two weeks. I mean, the stats—"

Conrad held up a hand to interrupt. "I know you have, Gord, but you have to look at this from a scouting perspective. You're four to five years older than most of the hitters in this league. Plus, you have four years of college ball under your belt. You're getting these guys out with maturity and guile, not with your stuff. These guys are still too raw to know what pitches to hit and what pitches to lay off. You've just been taking advantage of that—as you should. But that won't work in Double A. The hitters are much smarter up there. They'd use you as batting practice. I'm sorry, Gord, I really am."

Gord looked at his manager. Conrad appeared to have aged fifteen years over the course of their brief conversation.

Gord felt zero sympathy for him. *He feels bad. What about how I feel?* Gord thought. *He still has a job. He's still involved in the game.*

Gord wanted answers. "Well, what the fuck am I supposed to do now, Tom?"

Conrad sat silent. Invariably, every player he released showed flashes of anger when faced with his baseball mortality. There was nothing Conrad could say to defuse the anger, so he usually kept his mouth shut and let the player vent.

A deep pit of rage and frustration boiled through Gord. He bolted upright, knocking his chair over in the process. "Well? Come on. You seem to have all the fucking answers," he shouted. "What am I supposed to do now? I've wanted to play baseball since I was five fucking years old. And you're telling me I can't anymore. How is that right? Who made you God?"

Gord turned away from his manager. Yelling and screaming wasn't going to change his mind. Nothing would. Gord's professional baseball dream was over. Blinking through tears, he looked back at Conrad. The shouting was replaced with a whisper. "What am I going to do?"

"I've watched you over the past year. Not just on the field, but off. In the clubhouse, on the bus during road trips. I've seen the way guys on the team look at you. They respond to you. You were a leader on this team. You showed a lot of these young guys how to prepare for games and act like a professional. They saw you in here busting your tail in the weight room, pouring every last ounce of blood, sweat, and tears into making yourself a better pitcher."

"Yeah, well, apparently it wasn't enough," Gord bitterly retorted.

"Maybe not, but as a manager, your heart and determination was a privilege to witness. You're part of a dying breed, Gord. A true student of the game. There aren't many of us left. Most of the pitchers on my staff owe you a debt of gratitude for helping them with their command, or their breaking stuff, or the polish necessary to thrive in the face of adversity."

Conrad let his words linger in the air for a moment before he continued.

"Earlier today, I called Hank Walton, the manager in Erie. I wanted an update on Johnson, to see how he was doing. The kid is on fire up there. Lights out. Not only that, but he's started lifting weights and has really committed himself to his bullpen sessions between starts. He's reading scouting reports and watching videos of his mechanics. Anything he can do to get better.

"I asked Hank what catalyzed the change. Apparently, Danny

said it was a conversation the two of you had before he left. He said you challenged him to reach his potential. That you showed him how to get the most of his talent. You're a natural teacher, Gord."

"Look, Tom. That's great. I'm really happy for Danny," Gord said. "But that still doesn't change the fact that my baseball career is over."

Conrad shook his head. "It doesn't have to be. You can still be a part of the game. Have you ever thought about coaching?"

"I'm twenty-four years old, Tom. You want me to staple my ass to a bench and write out lineup cards?"

"No. I mean as an instructor. You have the knowledge and demeanour to teach pitching. Any organization would be lucky to have someone like you on their payroll, fine-tuning the deliveries of their draft picks."

"With all due respect, Tom, I don't think that's for me. I couldn't stand teaching guys to pitch when, in my heart, I know I can still throw at this level. The Wildcats may think my career is over, but I don't."

"I respect that, Gord. And I wish you the best of luck. It has been a pleasure having you on the squad."

"Thanks, Tom."

The two men shook hands across Conrad's desk. Gord left the office quietly. He had walked into the office supremely confident and in possession of an impressive scoreless innings streak. He left the office with an outright release and a shattered baseball career.

In a daze, Gord made his way across the width of the clubhouse. Not wanting to begin the agonizing process of cleaning out his locker, Gord sat shell-shocked in front of it. He struggled to grasp the stupefying reality of his release.

"What did Conrad want?" asked a smirking Chris Seaboard. "Do we have to cover your ass with rose petals when you go into the shower now?"

Gord didn't even acknowledge his teammate's presence. It was like he didn't know Seaboard was there.

"Jesus, what's wrong with you?" Seaboard continued. "Your face is white as a sheet." He snapped his fingers a foot from Gord's face.

Gord peered at Seaboard. "I'm done."

"You're done? Done what? What does that mean?"

"I'm done. Cut. Released."

"Fuck off," Seaboard cracked, thinking Gord was putting him on.

Gord shook his head sadly. "That's what Conrad wanted to see me about."

"Jesus Christ." Seaboard sat down beside him. "Why?"

"Because I'm a dinosaur, man. I'm too old for A ball and the front office doesn't project me to get promoted. So, I'm gone. They're making room for the new crop of arms."

"Fuck, man, I'm so sorry."

"Hey, boys. What's up?" Steve Anderson strolled into the clubhouse. He approached Gord and Seaboard.

The silence was deafening. Seaboard awkwardly averted his eyes from Anderson, unwilling to be the bearer of bad news. Gord glanced up at his fellow pitcher.

"I just got released."

"What?" inquired a disbelieving Anderson. "You're kidding me?"

By the looks on their faces, it was clear to Anderson that Gord wasn't kidding.

"That's so shitty."

Nodding, Gord stood up and wordlessly stuffed the contents of his locker into a large, black duffel bag. He worked at a feverish pace, wishing to speed up the inevitable and get away from two dozen sets of prying eyes. Gord knew that, as soon as he left, gossip and rumours of his dismissal would fly furiously around the clubhouse. He turned back to his visibly uncomfortable bullpen mates.

"Look, guys, I don't want to make this any tougher than it is. I'll always consider both of you great friends and I hope both of you make it to the Show." He embraced both Seaboard and Anderson.

"I'll miss you guys." Gord struggled to keep his composure. "I better go make my rounds."

Slinging the duffel bag over his right shoulder, Gord made his way around the clubhouse and said goodbye to the rest of the Wildcats milling around their lockers. His departure caught the majority of the team off-guard.

Gord's release was taken harder by a lot of the guys than one might think. And it had nothing to do with Gord's popularity in the clubhouse. Gord's exodus actually made a lot of the Wildcats question their own baseball mortality. *If it could happen to him, it could happen to me*, they thought.

Baseball was a fickle game. One minute you could be a star on a meteoric rise to the top—the next minute, you could be on your way out of town with a one-way bus ticket. The privilege of playing baseball for a living was not something to be taken for granted, and sometimes it took the release of a teammate to remember that.

Amidst the melancholic atmosphere of Gord's farewell was a moment of levity provided by Tyson Dante.

Dante was in the stadium's indoor cage taking extra batting practice when word of Gord's release reached him. Dante stormed out of the cage and found Gord just as he was preparing to leave the clubhouse for the last time.

"Gord!"

He turned to face the diminutive slugger.

"You're gone?" Dante asked.

"Yeah," Gord replied.

Dante was silent for a moment. "Shit, you can't go," he whined. "I'm hitting .500 in the games you pitch!"

Gord's lips curled up in a slight smile. "I think I'm going to miss you most of all, Scarecrow."

"What does that mean?" Dante was confused. "I don't understand."

"Exactly. See you later, Tyson."

Gord walked out of the clubhouse. For the first time in his life, he couldn't call himself a baseball player. He didn't know what he was.

# September 2008

## Orlando, Florida

"I'm running out of options, here, Kim." Gord was despondent.

The only sound in Kim's condo was the lake breeze sauntering in from the balcony and gently whipping the blinds against the sliding glass door.

Nursing a beer, Gord sat defeated in the middle of Kim's loveseat with his feet propped up on an ottoman. Kim sat perpendicular to him on the couch, her feet tucked beneath her legs.

"There's no one else you can contact?" she queried.

"I've called everyone I can think of. They all told me the same thing the Wildcats did. No one wants a twenty-four-year-old middle reliever clogging up a roster spot in A ball."

It had been two weeks since Gord's release from the Wildcats' organization. Since then, he had spent each day calling every friend, colleague, and acquaintance he had in professional baseball, asking—make that begging—for a roster spot. Every reply was the same. *We'd love to help you, Gord, but we don't have the room, money, or need for your services.*

"Besides, it's Labour Day weekend now," Gord continued. "The chances of finding something at this point in the season are slim to none. I can't get a spot in the Instructional League without a minor league contract and I don't have the juice or cachet behind my name to play winter ball."

Kim took a deep breath. She had a suggestion, but it was unlikely to be well-received by Gord. She knew she had to tread carefully when broaching the subject.

"Well, maybe it's time to start thinking about life after baseball. Like what do you want to do, career-wise?"

"Life after baseball? All I've ever wanted to do is play the game for a living. What else can I do?"

"You have your kinesiology degree . . ." Kim let her words linger, giving Gord the opportunity to fill in his own ending.

"So, you think I should be a gym teacher?"

"Not necessarily—" she started to reply, but Gord cut her off.

"No, yeah, that's a good idea," Gord quipped. "I can buy a pair of nice, tight cotton shorts, wear knee-high socks, grow a moustache, and have a whistle dangle permanently from my neck. Then I can berate a group of twenty-five eight-year-olds for not running fast enough from point A to point B. Sounds like a very rewarding career."

"Look, Gord," Kim's eyes flashed with anger. "I am sorry that baseball isn't working out for you right now. But I'm trying to help you to get through this. I don't need to put up with your pity party, woe is me, sarcastic bullshit."

She spat out the last two syllables and stormed out to the balcony. *Fuck, I shouldn't have said that,* Gord thought. *She's right. Man up and stop acting like a petulant asshole.*

Gord took the last swig of his beer and placed the bottle on the glass coffee table. He followed Kim to the balcony.

"Kim, I'm sorry. I'm just having a hard time with this. But that still doesn't give me the right to take my frustration out on you." He put his hands on her shoulders as she faced Lake Lucerne. "Having you with me is what's getting me through this. I'd be going nuts without you."

Kim smiled and turned to face him. "Well, I guess you're not as dumb as you look."

Gord kissed her. With their foreheads pressed together, Gord revealed what else had been bothering him the past week.

"I haven't told my dad about my release yet."

Michael Mattis had followed his son's professional career with the same fervour that he had during Gord's high school and college years. But with Gord plying his trade in Florida and Michael remaining in Michigan, he was forced to follow the Lakeland Wildcats in absentia.

Michael constantly scoured the Internet for stat updates and listened to every game he could on satellite radio. He had messaged Gord a few days earlier, inquiring about his disappearance from the team's box scores over the last fourteen days.

Gord hastily created a fake hamstring injury to mollify his snooping father, but he knew he couldn't depend on the pulled muscle for very much longer.

"How do you think he'll react?" Kim asked. She was concerned, as she knew about their somewhat fractured past.

"I have no idea, but most likely some degree of furious."

Michael's hard-assed approach to the game and relentless pushing of his son to greater heights had waned slightly since Gord got drafted. Gord surmised it was because he had reached a higher level than his father. Thus, Gord had surpassed Michael's decidedly high expectations for his son.

That being said, Michael still demanded the best from Gord. Poor pitching performances were usually followed by tersely worded notes offering "suggestions" for improvement. Oddly enough, the better Gord pitched, the less he heard from his father. Silence was the sincerest form of flattery in Michael Mattis's motivational handbook.

"When were you planning on calling?"

"I wanted to wait until I exhausted all of my possibilities. Since I've pretty much done that, I've just kept trying to put it off. I am not looking forward to that conversation." Gord paused and leaned over the balcony, inhaling the sweet Florida air.

"You can do it here, if you want." Kim put a comforting hand on his shoulder. "I can give you some moral support."

Gord was nervous. How could he tell his dad that the dream both of them had shared since Gord was a kid had come to an end? *What do I say? How do I start?*

"Thanks. I should just do it now. Otherwise, this is going to be eating me up inside until I call." Gord looked intently at Kim. "But this is something I have to do by myself."

She hugged him. "I understand. You can have the place to yourself. I have to go out shopping anyway." She kissed Gord on the cheek. "Good luck."

Gord paced around the condo with Kim's cordless phone in his hand. He whacked it on the back of his neck, rehearsing various scenarios on how to break the news. When he finally came up with something half-decent, he dialled his father's number. Shaking with trepidation, he tried to calm his breathing as he listened to a third ring.

"Hello?"

"Hey, Dad."

"Gordon," his father panted. "How are you?"

"I'm doing okay." Gord paused, concerned. "Are you okay? Why are you breathing so hard?"

"Yeah, I'm fine. Just got back from a run."

"Oh, okay."

Silence lingered over the connection. Gord internally waged a back-and-forth battle over whether or not to tell his father. *I'll let him bring it up,* Gord decided. *Maybe he won't ask about baseball,* he foolishly hoped.

Sure enough, his son's baseball career had the pole position in Michael's mind.

"How's the hamstring?"

"It's not too bad. It's still pretty tender."

"Have you been rehabbing? It's been what, two and a half weeks since your last appearance? If you can throw, you should throw." Michael lectured. "You don't need to be 100 percent. You don't want the team to think you're flaky or soft."

*Yeah, thanks for the concern, there, Pops.* Gord shook his head. *This is going to be tougher than I thought.*

"Plus, you seemed to have turned a corner just before you got hurt," Michael continued. "You were throwing the way you're capable of instead of getting lit up all over the park. It reminded me of the way you threw in college."

*I think there was a compliment sandwiched in there somewhere. Okay, you have him on the phone, just tell him. He's going to find out eventually. I can't have a pulled hamstring for the rest of my life.*

"Listen, Dad. The truth is my hamstring is fine. I was never hurt."

"What?" A considerable edge infiltrated his father's voice.

"I had to make it up. That was the only way to cover for the real reason why I haven't been on the active roster for the past couple of weeks."

"Why haven't you played? What did you do?"

"I didn't DO *any*thing," Gord retorted defensively.

"What the hell are you talking about?"

Gord audibly sighed over the phone. "I got released."

"What?" Michael was incredulous. "You got cut?"

"Yes."

Gord braced himself for the explosion that was sure to come. He figured his father would upbraid him like a marine drill sergeant admonishing a recruit for falling behind on a run. Michael was pissed, of that there was no doubt. However, to the surprise of his son, the target of his anger was not Gord, but, instead, the Detroit organization.

"Why did they cut you?" he thundered.

"They basically told me I'm too old to be a prospect. They didn't see me going higher than A ball, so there was no point of having me on the team clogging up a roster spot for a guy with a bigger upside."

"That is total bullshit!" Michael shouted. "You were the best pitcher they had for a month! Plus, a scoreless innings streak that was longer than anyone else's on the staff. And you're the only left-hander they have in the bullpen. That's a horrible baseball decision."

"Uh, yeah."

Gord was speechless. Flabbergasted might be a better word for it. He had never heard his father directly praise him for his work on the baseball field. Even in college, when Gord was the ace of the staff, Michael never gave pure congratulations for Gord's performances. It was always "Not bad, but . . ." "Pretty good, but next time . . ." There was always qualifying criticism to any semblance of a compliment.

It was a tremendous surprise to hear his dad say that he was the best pitcher on Lakeland's staff, but even more so to hear how closely Michael followed the team. He must have dissected each game's stats and completely devoured the box scores. That's the only way Michael would have known about the scoreless innings streak to begin with, let alone know where it ranked among the rest of the staff. Gord knew that his dad followed his career, but he had no idea that it was to such an extent.

"You know what, forget about the Wildcats. There are plenty of other teams out there. You should get on the phone and start looking for other possible spots."

"Yeah, I know, Dad." Gord said curtly. He was angry that his father thought he'd been sitting on his ass doing nothing for the past two weeks. "I've called everyone I can think of."

"And?"

"And they've all told me the same thing the Wildcats did. No one wants a twenty-four-year-old pitcher in A ball. I waited so long to call you because I wanted to make sure I'd explored all my options. I don't know what else to do. This looks like it's the e—" He choked on the word "end." He didn't want to say it out loud.

"What about next year? Maybe you can get a non-roster invite to spring training? You could really commit yourself to training harder than ever in the off-season."

"That's not going to work. No one invites unsigned A ball players to spring training. Those spots are for older guys from the majors looking to reclaim past glory. Or for guys from Triple A on the cusp of the Show. It's not for situational lefties cut from the Central Florida League."

"Well, if this is truly the end of your career, I just want you to know that—" Something caught in Michael's throat as he struggled to find the right words to say to his son.

He soldiered on. "I just want you to know that you being drafted and playing professional baseball has been the proudest moment of my life."

"Dad?"

"I know I was hard on you growing up. I pushed you harder than I should have, but it's just—I just wanted you to reach your potential. The potential I always believed that you had. I know I've never told you that before and that's my fault."

"I—"

Michael cut him off. "Just let me finish." Michael was purging his soul, telling his son things he had wanted to say years ago, but didn't—or couldn't.

"I like to think that my pushing and prodding is what inspired you to become a better pitcher. Was it the right way to go about things? Probably not. Should I have been more supportive? Yes, but I didn't know any other way. Your effort and accomplishments are all due to your hard work and determination. Maybe I provided the fire and was the catalyst, but you had a dream and you went out there and got it. Not many people can say that. So, you're not going to make the big leagues? It's not the end of the world. You had the opportunity to play baseball for a living. There are thousands of kids who would give anything to say they had the baseball career you did. You strived for excellence and you achieved it."

"It means a lot to me to hear you say that." An invisible weight was lifted off Gord's shoulders. "I think deep down I always knew you had my back and that you were proud of me. But, to actually hear you say those words, it—it means a lot to me."

"I am proud of you. I always have been. I think back to when you were a teenager and how much it hurt you to struggle at the game. It broke me up inside. I just wanted you to be happy and have the success I know you deserved. All of the shit I gave you over the years—the criticisms, the suggestions, the critiques. They were all from a place of tough love. I love you, son."

The last sentence crackled through the long distance connection. Those four words instantly melted away the hundreds of miles of figurative and literal distance between father and son.

Gord could hardly believe his ears. He had never heard his father say that to him before. Ironically, the end of Gord's baseball career had actually brought the two Mattis men closer together.

"I love you too, Dad."

"And whatever you choose to do with your life or whatever path you decide to take, always know that I am behind you one hundred percent. You'll figure this out, Gord. You're a fighter."

"Thanks."

"You take care of yourself."

"You too. 'Bye, Dad."

"'Bye, son."

# March 2009

## Lakeland, Florida
## Mercantile Stadium

"I don't know about this, Kim."

"Gord, you've put this off long enough. We're here; we might as well go."

They stood in the parking lot adjacent to Mercantile Stadium amidst a sea of cars. Gord hesitated at the driver's side of his champagne-coloured coupe. It was the last week of spring training before the big club headed north to Detroit for the start of the regular season.

Gord was only at the stadium because of repeated requests by his former roommate, Danny Johnson. Johnson was invited to major league spring training by the front office as a reward for his terrific season the year before. Still a teenager, Johnson had no real shot of making the big club, but the experience of being around the team for a few weeks would be instrumental for his development as a professional.

Danny had deluged Gord with a barrage of phone calls and emails all month. He wanted Gord to attend one of his spring training appearances before he was sent back to Double A to begin the regular season. Gord had declined all previous invites because he figured the wounds would be too fresh and raw to step back into the place where he saw his own dream snuffed out.

One last attempt by Danny, and some gentle prodding from Kim, had catalyzed Gord's appearance at his last start with the big leaguers. Danny was scheduled to throw seventy-five pitches in that afternoon's contest against Toronto. If he pitched well, Danny would end up throwing about six innings.

While there were dozens of cars in the parking lot, it was completely devoid of people as Gord and Kim made the long walk to the stadium entrance. It was just before two in the afternoon. The game had started at one o'clock. Gord wanted to sneak in and sit high in the bleachers, far from the action. He didn't want to risk the very small chance that he might be recognized by a Lakeland mega-fan or a stadium employee.

Gord and Kim stood in the main concourse of the stadium. The gentle sounds of spring baseball echoed throughout the concrete structure. They couldn't yet see the vivid green and brown of the playing surface, but Gord visibly stiffened as they got closer.

"Are you okay?" Kim asked.

"Yeah, I think so."

"You sure you're ready to do this?"

"Well, I have to eventually." Gord steeled himself. "I might as well get it over with now."

"I'm here if you need me," Kim replied sweetly, grasping Gord's hand to emphasize her point.

They walked hand-in-hand to the field. This was the first time in years that Gord had seen a game from the stands. He was awed at the beauty that lay before him. There was nothing like the first glance of the season at a perfectly manicured baseball diamond. For a fan of the game, it was akin to a religious experience.

Gord and Kim found their seats forty rows behind Toronto's dugout and settled in to watch the home half of the third inning. The small, plastic seats made a comfortable seating experience all but impossible. As his vibrating knees could attest, Gord was jittery and anxious as the Detroit hitters dug in at the plate.

He had prepared himself for a difficult afternoon. He assumed it would be tremendously difficult and emotional to watch people—his former colleagues—play the game he loved. Kim placed a hand on Gord's left knee to calm his frayed nerves.

Grateful for her presence, Gord gave Kim a meek smile as the sharp crack of a batted ball snapped both of their heads toward the field. As Toronto's third baseman scooped up the hard-hit ground ball, an odd revelation washed over Gord.

*This isn't that bad*, he thought. Surprised at his admission, Gord focused on the action. He studied the position players and watched the rhythmic dance of each at-bat. Still, nothing. All of his nervousness and anxiety just melted away.

Gord found himself actually enjoying the game as a fan. *Why?*

*What was going on?* Could the seven months since his release have healed his pain?

"I'm going to grab a beer. Do you want one?" Kim inquired.

"That'd be great. Thanks. You want me to come with you?"

"No, you stay here. I'll be right back." She kissed him on the cheek and trekked down toward the concession stand.

Gord allowed himself to relax slightly. *I assumed this would have been worse,* he thought. *Why I am doing so well? Were all my concerns for naught?*

*Wait,* he stopped himself. *I don't know any of the players currently on the field. I don't have any memories with these guys. Right now, it's just another baseball game. Once Danny comes out of the dugout, everything will come flooding back. I don't think I can handle that.*

The third inning ended with Detroit stranding runners at second and third. Gord looked around. *I hope Kim gets back soon.* Gord's breath began to quicken as he waited for Danny to emerge from the dugout.

*Maybe I'll go see if Kim needs some help,* he cowardly decided. He hustled down the bleachers and disappeared into the concourse just as Danny sprinted to the mound. Gord nearly ran Kim over as he jogged toward the beer concession.

"What are you doing?" Kim cried. She narrowly avoided showering herself with two cups of beer.

"I, uh, just wanted to see if you needed some help," Gord replied sheepishly.

"Right." She rolled her eyes. "Well, you might as well take these now."

Kim handed Gord the tray and led them back to their seats. Danny had just completed his warm-up pitches in the top of the fourth. He stood behind the mound waiting for the ball to be tossed back to him.

Gord leaned forward in his seat, his elbows propped up on his knees and his hands covering his mouth. He watched Danny confidently accept his catcher's sign and deliver a darting fastball over the inner half of the plate. Strike one.

Oddly, Gord felt somewhat detached from the scene down on the field. He didn't feel like he was missing anything watching Danny pitch. He didn't have any feelings of remorse or bitter pangs of jealousy. Instead, he appreciated the game from a fan's perspective. *I still love the game,* he realized.

Watching Danny carve up the Toronto hitters—many of whom were established members of the major league roster—only reinforced the discrepancies between Gord's talent level and Johnson's otherworldly abilities. It was really that simple. Gord didn't have the stuff to make it to the Show. Danny did. Gord had squeezed every last ounce of talent and ability out of his body. He had nothing to be ashamed of.

The emotional turmoil that had threatened to ruin his afternoon had dissipated like the morning fog on a spring afternoon. Instead, Gord marvelled at the command and surgical precision of Danny's pitching repertoire.

"I can't believe how well he's throwing. It's such a huge difference from last year," Gord told Kim as Danny set down Toronto in order in the fourth.

He had spun four scoreless innings to that point. He had struck out five, walked none, and had only relinquished two hits.

Kim looked at Gord quizzically. "I thought you said he was the best pitcher on your team last year. How can he be throwing so much better now?"

Gord smiled. To the untrained eye, it did look like Danny was dominating the hitters with similar ease to the year before. However, as a pitcher, Gord detected slight nuances in Danny's delivery and execution. These nuances were proof that the young fireballer was light-years ahead in his development since Gord last saw him pitch.

"Watch him next inning. Last year, he just used his natural ability to get guys out. Now, he's using his brain to get hitters out. He's not sacrificing control for strikeouts. Every pitch he threw that inning had a purpose. It's like a game of chess. Each pitch sets up a subsequent pitch. He's toying with the batters, thinking two to three pitches ahead. He's getting inside their heads, disrupting their timing. His delivery looks more polished and refined, too. His plant foot lands in the exact same spot every pitch. Last year, he couldn't replicate that delivery—which sometimes got him into trouble."

Kim looked at him like he was speaking in tongues. "You're such a nerd," she teased.

Danny came out for the top of the fifth inning and continued his stellar outing. He threw with a poise and maturity well beyond his years. After the first batter struck out on a 2–2 count, Gord turned to Kim excitedly. "He's throwing slower than last year, too."

"Why is that a good thing?"

"Instead of trying to throw as hard as he can on every pitch, he can be just as effective by taking a few clicks off the speedometer and emphasizing control and movement. That will make hitters put a few more balls in play, which will lower his pitch count. It will allow him to throw deeper into games, with less stress on his arm. But, if he needs a big strikeout, he can always reach back for a little something extra. It usually takes young guys with big fastballs years to learn such restraint and put a premium on finesse instead of power. The fact Danny appears to have it down now is a scary, scary thought."

Kim flashed Gord a sarcastic grin. "You're getting overstimulated. Should I be worried about the two of you?"

"Shut up," Gord replied playfully.

After the game, Gord and Kim waited for Danny outside of the players' entrance. There was a smattering of fans waiting for autographs from the handful of Detroit stars in the game. Danny emerged from the stadium and was immediately hounded by . . . no one.

The big club's franchise player had left the clubhouse a few seconds earlier and drawn the attention of the autograph-seeking horde. Danny worked his way through the crowd unmolested and broke into a huge grin when he spotted Gord and Kim standing on the periphery.

"Gordo!" Danny exclaimed. "Good to see you, buddy!"

He dropped his bag and moved toward Gord with his arms outstretched. The two former roommates embraced in a back-slapping man-hug.

"Danny Boy! It's been a while." Gord took a step back and gave Danny a quick once-over.

"What are you looking at?"

"It looks like you've put on a little beef. Welcome to an adult body weight, pal."

"Fuck you!" Danny retorted. "We're starting this already?"

Gord shrugged his shoulders. "That's what we do, Bonus Baby."

Danny noticed Kim standing at Gord's side. "You must be Kim!" He thrust his right hand toward her.

"Nice to meet you, Danny."

"Likewise. What do you see in him?" he asked, jerking his thumb in Gord's direction. "You are way out of his league."

Kim nodded in agreement. "I tell him that every day."

Gord rolled his eyes. "Please don't encourage him."

"Too late," Danny quipped. "Where are we going to eat? I'm starving."

"Road House Bar?"

"Sweet. The waitresses there are so hot." He paused, scanning the parking lot. "Where are you parked?"

"Over there," Gord replied, pointing to the southeast corner of the lot.

Danny took off in the direction of Gord's finger as Gord and Kim dutifully followed.

"So, I figure they'll start me in Double A, but if I keep throwing like today I could see being moved up to Triple A by the first day of summer," Danny said between bites of a gigantic platter of chicken wings. "And, fingers crossed, maybe a promotion to the Show for an outing or two once rosters expand in September."

"That's great. I'm really happy for you."

Danny sucked back the rest of his pint and signalled their waitress to bring them another pitcher of beer. "What are you doing now, Gordo?"

"I'm in school at the University of Central Florida."

"Really?"

"Yeah, I'm going for my doctorate in Physical Therapy."

"Jesus, that's impressive. What are you looking to do with that?"

"The doctorate, plus my kinesiology degree, should give me a bunch of options once I graduate. I've been thinking about specializing in rehabbing athletes from injuries, and maybe focusing on increased athletic performance. But, I'd also like to help the elderly and infirm increase their functional capabilities. Help them maintain a great quality of life."

"Wow." Danny was stunned to hear his former roommate's commitment to higher education. "Where'd you get that idea from?"

"Actually, it was Kim's idea." Gord smiled appreciatively at his girlfriend.

"I figured as much.

"Actually, Kim," Danny began, his face scrunched up in thought. "I wanted to ask you something, it's been bugging me ever since we met. I know I've seen you somewhere before, but I just can't place it. What do you do for a living?"

"I'm an entertainment reporter for Channel 13."

"That's it!" He slapped the table. "I knew you looked familiar. You do celebrity gossip, dating-type stuff, right?"

"Yep. I'm hoping to move to an anchor role soon."

Danny whistled. "Smart, fun, a TV personality, and an absolute rocket."

Kim grinned mischievously at Gord. "I like this guy."

"Gordo, you have to lock her down."

"I'm working on it."

The three of them laughed. Gord refilled their glasses with the fresh pitcher of beer. Danny took a long pull from his glass. He looked at Gord and turned uncharacteristically serious.

"Do you, uh, miss the game at all?"

Gord cleared his throat and shifted in his chair. "The end of last season was really tough. The fall and winter were fine, but I don't usually think too much about baseball during the off-season anyway. We'll see how this spring is, though. That's why it took me so long to come and watch you. I wasn't sure if I could handle it."

"How was it?"

"Honestly, it wasn't too bad. But it's only March. Time will tell what April brings and my body and mind realize that I haven't thrown yet. And that I won't be throwing."

"That makes sense."

Danny delivered his next words methodically, like he had rehearsed them in his mind. "The main reason I wanted you to come watch me pitch is that I wanted you to know how important you have been to my career. I took my abilities for granted before. I thought I could just coast by on natural talent. You showed me that I shouldn't let anything go to waste. How to physically and mentally prepare for starts. You showed me how to become a pitcher and not just a thrower. How to use my brain when I'm on the bump. For that,

I'll always be grateful."

"It was my pleasure, Danny. You're going to be great. You have a chance to do something special with your career. I'm just glad I had the privilege of being a part of it. Now," Gord said, a shit-eating grin dancing across his face, "just make sure you remember me when you sign that first big contract."

"You got it, man," Danny laughed. "What are you two doing to-night? Staying in town?"

"No, we're heading back to Orlando tonight. I have to study, and Kim's working tomorrow."

"Too bad, we could have painted the town for old time's sake." Danny glanced around the Road House Bar. "I wonder what time our waitress gets off. Maybe she's up for a little *fun* tonight."

"I'm pretty sure she's wearing a wedding ring," Kim offered.

"That's okay," Danny smiled. "I like a challenge." He stood up and went to proposition the unsuspecting woman as she entered orders at the service terminal.

Kim gave Gord a confused look. "He's kidding, right?"

He smiled. "Absolutely not."

# April 2009

## Orlando, Florida

Gord stirred slightly in bed. The warm embrace of the Florida sun comforted his naked torso like a hot towel fresh out of the dryer. He stretched his arms out in front of him and clasped his hands behind his head.

He slowly opened his eyes. He was completely refreshed and rested.

Gord reached for his cell phone. He was careful not to disturb Kim, who slept soundly beside him. He checked the time. Eight o'clock. He placed the phone back on the nightstand. The prospect of more uninterrupted sleep called his head back to the pillow on this lazy Saturday morning.

Suddenly, Gord stopped himself. With a furrowed brow, he reached for his phone once again. This time Gord checked the date. April 10.

Perplexed, Gord struggled to comprehend the significance of the date. His subconscious was trying to tell him something. Slowly, he began to put the pieces together.

It was April. Already. Baseball season. Gord never slept well during the spring and summer. What was different? *I haven't thrown since last August*, he realized. That was the longest stretch of his life since he first picked up a ball.

But that wasn't all. Something else was different. Something was missing. *What was it?* The revelation smacked him in the face. *The dream. The dream was gone.*

Gord wasn't sure how to feel. The dream had always been both a blessing and a curse. He had always defined himself by baseball. The dream reminded him of that. Without the game, Gord thought he'd be lost. Like a man without a purpose.

But he didn't feel lost at all. He felt good. Content. Completely at ease. Never again would he be visited by the dream. It wasn't a part of his life anymore. Gord smiled. He felt Kim move beside him.

"What is it, Gord?" she asked groggily.

"I just realized that—it's, uh, nothing."

"You sure? You can tell me."

"I just realized how happy I am right now. With you. At this point in my life. I think it just took me a little while to fully appreciate it."

She smiled. "Good."

"Go back to sleep," he whispered.

Gord realized he didn't need baseball to be happy. True happiness required more than just a glove and a ball. He leaned over and kissed Kim on the cheek. Wrapping his arms around her, Gord closed his eyes and drifted off to sleep.

# About the Author

(BROWN'S PHOTOS)

Mike Arsenault played semi-professional baseball for the London Majors of the Intercounty Baseball League. He learned to play the game from an early age growing up in Oshawa, Ontario, Canada. A southpaw, Mike played on the varsity baseball team at both Queen's University and Durham College and was named pitcher of the year three times in five years.

Currently, Mike works as a freelance reporter/photographer and television host. He also hosts a sports/pop culture podcast and has a few acting credits under his belt. This is his first novel.

For more information on Mike's media endeavours, visit *www.mikegarsenault.blogspot.com* or follow him on Twitter @MikeGArsenault.

TO ORDER MORE COPIES:

GSPH

General Store Publishing House
499 O'Brien Road, Box 415, Renfrew, Ontario, Canada K7V 4A6
Tel 1.800.465.6072 • Fax 1.613.432.7184
www.gsph.com

VISA MasterCard